LIBRARY TRAINING GUIDES

Series Editor: David Baker
Editorial Assistant: Joan Welsby

Other Library Training Guides available

Training needs analysis
Michael Williamson
1-85604-077-1

Induction
Julie Parry
1-85604-078-X

Evaluation
Steve Phillips
1-85604-079-8

Training and development for women
Beryl Morris
1-85604-080-1

Interpersonal skills
Philippa Levy
1-85604-081-X

Management of training and staff development
June Whetherly
1-85604-104-2

Mentoring
Biddy Fisher
1-85604-105-0

Recruitment
Julie Parry
1-85604-106-9

Supporting adult learners
Tony Bamber *et al.*
1-85604-125-5

Presenting information
Clare Nankivell and Michael Shoolbred
1-85604-125-5

Introduction by the Series Editor

This new series of Library Training Guides (LTGs for short) aims to fill the gap left by the demise of the old Training Guidelines published in the 1980s in the wake of The Library Association's work on staff training. The new LTGs develop the original concept of concisely written summaries of the best principles and practice in specific areas of training by experts in the field which give library and information workers a good-quality guide to best practice. Like the original guidelines, the LTGs also include appropriate examples from a variety of library systems as well as further reading and useful contacts.

Though each guide stands in its own right, LTGs form a coherent whole. Acquisition of all LTGs as they are published will result in a comprehensive manual of training and staff development in library and information work.

The guides are aimed at practising librarians and library training officers. They are intended to be comprehensive without being over-detailed; they should give both the novice and the experienced librarian/training officer an overview of what should/could be done in a given situation and in relation to a particular skill/group of library staff/type of library.

David Baker

LIBRARY TRAINING GUIDES

Personal Professional Development and the Solo Librarian

Sue Lacey Bryant

Library Association Publishing

© Library Association Publishing 1995

Published by
Library Association Publishing
7 Ridgmount Street
London WC1E 7AE

Except as otherwise permitted under the Copyright Designs and Patents Act 1988 this publication may only be reproduced, stored or transmitted in any form or by any means, with the prior permission of the publishers, or, in the case of reprographic reproduction, in accordance with the terms of a licence issued by The Copyright Licensing Agency. Enquiries concerning reproduction outside those terms should be sent to Library Association Publishing Ltd, 7 Ridgmount Street, London WC1E 7AE.

First published 1995

British Library Cataloguing in Publication Data.

A catalogue record for this book is available from the British Library.

ISBN 1-85604-141-7

Typeset in 11/12pt Palermo by Library Association Publishing
Printed and made in Great Britain by Amber (Printwork) Ltd, Harpenden, Herts.

Contents

Introduction

Personal professional development cannot be bought 'off-the-peg' – it has to be tailor-made, patterned to meet individual needs, and woven from the rich tapestry of life.

This practical guide meets the challenge of personal professional development. The systematic approach recommended here is applicable to librarians and information scientists working in organizations of every size, in every sector. Thus, although the guide addresses the specific needs of the growing number of information specialists who work solo, or with minimal help, it will also be of interest to every information worker with a personal commitment to professional development.

1.1 Personal professional development

I use the terms Personal, Professional and Development in the following sense:

- *personal*: relating primarily to the needs of the individual, rather than those of the employing organization, and concerned with deliberate self-development which, although self-directed, cannot be accomplished alone;
- *professional*: concerned with the specialized knowledge and skills, and those attitudes, standards and values which together contribute to competence in the conduct of our vocation;
- *development*: reflecting a dynamic continuous process of growth and achievement, in which a willingness to change is inherent.

Personal Professional Development is just that: a personal responsibility. It is one which solo information workers are well able to shoulder, harnessing the same resourcefulness which equips them to enjoy the challenge of providing an information service single-handed to identifying, planning and using opportunities for their own development.

A 'confusion of terminology'[1] within education and training circles, among employers and within the wider profession, has tended to obscure the issue of responsibility and how it should be shared, thus slowing the profession's response to the challenges of continuing professional development. Anyone who wishes to explore these issues further is directed to the section on Professional Development in the Select Bibliography.

1.2 The solo librarian

I use the term *solo librarian* to embrace all those librarians, information scientists, and information workers who manage information units on their own, or who work as the sole professional, providing a library and information service with the minimum of support. The development of the concept of solo information work has been outlined elsewhere by St Clair and Williamson (1992).[2]

It is evident that more and more people find themselves managing information services on their own: some attracted by the responsibility, independence and job satisfaction that such work can offer, some enticed by new information roles in the emerging market[3] (see section 2.1), and some left as the 'last Mohican' in a 'downsized' service.

Chapter 2 considers the number of information professionals now managing solo units, and the sectors in which they are employed.

1.3 Why bother with professional development?

Each information specialist will be led to plan and pursue professional development by highly personal motivators.

Personal reasons may include: ambition, boredom with 'the old routine', a desire for recognition, enthusiasm to learn, frustration, interest and self-interest, a search for fulfilment, a sense of isolation, a fear of obsolescence, panic, and the need to bolster self-confidence.

Professional reasons may include: commitment to high standards of service, concern to improve the performance of the unit and to prepare to meet future challenges, a desire for career advancement, job satisfaction, a wish to combat professional stagnation and, finally, recognition of the implications of change (particularly the diversification of information roles, the expansion of the knowledge base and the impact of new technology).

In response to the pace of economic, educational, social and technological changes, the professional associations now emphasize the need for continuing professional development. The largest professional body of library and information workers in the United Kingdom, The Library Association, requires that:

> Members must be competent in their professional activities including the requirement to keep abreast of developments in librarianship in those branches of professional practice in which qualifications and experience entitle them to engage.[4]

Continuing professional development is not 'a fringe activity', to quote Todd; rather 'it is one of the most important resources a professional can draw on to maintain competence'.[5]

1.4 What is needed?

There is a wealth of evidence and experience which illuminates the development needs of solo information workers as a group, in the light of which the individual can begin to assess personal development needs.

Even the most competent and confident manager of a one-person or one-professional unit will occasionally experience a sense of isolation. This takes two forms, described by Padden as a separation 'from professional developments, arguments and encouragement', and the absence of another professional who can 'appraise or criticise' professional development and 'on whom to test new ideas'.[6] Chapter 3 focuses on practical ways in which the solo professional can develop the 'invisible college' to overcome these difficulties.

The diversity of the responsibilities of the solo information worker, by contrast to the more specialized role of most peers in larger services, governs the wide nature of their need for continuing professional development. Chapter 4 explores the specific development needs of solo information workers in the context of the needs of employers and relevant research from the mainstream of library practice.

Self-motivation is the pivot upon which personal professional development rests, and there can be no other practitioner within the profession for whom self-motivation is more important than the solo librarian. Chapter 5 examines the significance of professional and personal values, the value of preparing a personal profile, and also introduces the concept of self-management by means of goal-setting.

1.4　How?

Many opportunities for professional development arise naturally within the workplace; some learning is intuitive, some lessons are salvaged from incidents which lead to a post-mortem, and much is achieved through reflection on past successes too.

In addition there is a wide range of informal and formal opportunities at work, and outside of it, for prospective learning, by means of experiences that can be planned in advance.

In Chapter 6 the advantages of completing a written plan, and documenting professional development in a personal portfolio, are considered. A systematic approach to drawing up a development plan is recommended. An evaluation of the information service plus a projection of its future needs, accompanied by an assessment of personal strengths and weaknesses, enables the information professional to identify goals for personal development.

Ironically, the difficulties which solo librarians and information workers commonly experience in attending formal events may encourage them to become more adept at exploiting a wider range of informal and work-based opportunities for personal development, and more eager to maximize the benefits of formal occasions, than many colleagues employed in the mainstream. Chapter 7 gives a comprehensive account of opportunities for personal professional development.

The pursuit of a further qualification creates opportunities which it is difficult to match by any other conventional form of continuing education. Chapter 8 reviews the pros and cons of investing in formal qualifications in librarianship and information work, pursuing professional qualifications, and studying for further qualifications.

1.6　How much?

Undue concern with the number of professional development activities engaged upon each year, rather than appraisal of the quality of what has been learnt is misleading. Instead, personal definition of specific, measurable goals gives a clear guide to achievement.

Nevertheless, managers of one-person and one-professional units often find themselves working alongside colleagues from other disciplines, who are subject to the requirements of their own professional bodies regarding continuing professional development. Accordingly it may be useful to note, and quote, that The Library Association recommends that the equivalent of 4-6 working days per annum should be devoted to activities which continue the individual's professional development.[7] Obviously it is not envisaged that all of this will be carried out during work-time.

1.7 What next?

Chapter 9 identifies factors which influence career advancement, considers the career patterns of solo librarians and information specialists, and discusses their career options.

Personal professional development should be the subject of continual review; flexibility in response to opportunity must be at its heart, and the improvement of professional practice its goal.

References

1   Roberts, N. and Konn, T., *Librarians and professional status: continuing professional development and academic libraries*, Library Association Publishing, 1991.
2   St Clair, G. and Williamson, J., *Managing the new one-person library*, 2nd edn, Bowker-Saur, 1992.
3   Moore, N., *The emerging markets for librarians and information workers*, British Library, 1987. Library and Information Research Report 56.
4   The Library Association, *The Library Association: code of professional conduct and guidance notes*, 2nd edn, 1995.
5   Todd, F. (ed.), *Planning continuing professional development*, Croom Helm, 1987.
6   Padden, S., 'The loneliness of the one-woman library', *Wilpower*, **33**, October 1986, 9-10.
7   The Library Association, *The framework for continuing professional development: your personal profile*, The Library Association, 1992.

2 Counting heads

The librarian or information officer managing a 'one-person' service is far from a rarity. Possibly as many as one in five qualified librarians and information workers in the United Kingdom work on their own, or with minimal support. However the paucity of sound statistical data is such that we are in the realms of 'best estimates' and surmise.

2.1 The size of the profession

The first stumbling block is to establish the number of people employed within library and information work.

The consultancy EUCLID, in an unpublished feasibility study for the Information and Library Services Lead Body in 1993, estimated a total workforce of 100,515 library and information workers, plus another 21,748 people undertaking some library duties in schools.[1]

The report highlights the fact that the Information and Library world has a 'moving front', characteristic of expanding industrial sectors.[2] New occupational territory is being opened up by those who exploit information as a management tool, and by those who 'produce' information.

2.1.1 Information professionals

The Library and Information Statistics Tables (THE L.I.S.T.)[3] gives a broad occupational overview based on 1992–3. It numbers 20,431 people in the profession, 17,067 of whom belong to either The Library Association or the Institute of Information Scientists or both.

The figures from the professional bodies are pretty much in line with this. The Library Association has around 25,000 members, of whom only some 16,000 currently work in the UK. The Institute of Information Scientists has some 2500 members and survey work at The Library Association[4] has suggested that one third (c.830) are likely to maintain dual membership. Although not everyone chooses to support professional associations, membership figures give some indication of the numbers who perceive themselves as active information professionals, irrespective of whether or not they hold qualifications in information science or librarianship.

2.2 The map of the profession

In which sectors do one-person and one-professional library and information services operate, and in which do they predominate? Consideration of these questions allows us to stand back from our own immediate specialism and reflect upon the different approaches that have emerged to serve the personal and professional development needs of personnel in each sector.

THE L.I.S.T.[5] offers the best starting point for a review of the number of 'lone' librarians.

- Almost all the 1070 schools librarians listed are employed as 'one-man bands' in secondary schools (and almost all are women).
- Of the 3862 librarians and information staff working in higher and further education, a small proportion (generally those employed within separate departments, faculties or institutes) feel an affinity with colleagues in 'one-professional' libraries.
- Similarly a very small number of the 7283 staff employed by public libraries may be lone operators, for instance prison librarians.
- Finally 7264 'special librarians' are listed, employed within industry and commerce, healthcare, government departments, the 'information industry' and miscellaneous other specialized services. Many manage information services on their own, or with little help.

It seems likely that some solo services, especially those staffed only on a part-time basis, do not appear in any of the statistics currently available.

2.3 UK special library statistics

In 1994 Berridge and Sumsion reported upon 'the disparate and generally weak' statistics available to describe the activity of 11 major sectors in the special library area.[6] Best estimates for 1993–4 show a total of 6922 professional librarians working in special libraries but the authors believe the 'Grand Total is probably still 5–10% understated'. Nevertheless the estimates show 4297 professional staff within industrial and commercial units, with another 2625 in 'other special libraries' – defined as government departments and agencies, local government, the National Health Service, professional societies, voluntary organizations and museums.

The three largest employers are in the industrial and commercial sector, namely pharmaceuticals, the media and law firms. Along with services offered by professional societies, these services are generally run by small teams of professional staff. Across the board, 80% of units (employing just half the 'Special Librarians') are staffed by an average of two professionals. The numbers vary from 1 in NHS libraries (in which 580 professionals are employed) through 1.5 in manufacturing industry (350 people), to 2.8 in banking and finance (466 people). A total of 3695 people work in these areas.

2.3.1 The 1972 and 1981 Census returns

Both Serjean's research on manpower planning (based on the 1972 Department of Education and Science Census of staff in librarianship and information work)[7] and East's review (of the 1981 Census)[8] showed that around 50% of special libraries in industry, commerce and government were one-person units.

This evidence of 'the preponderance of *small* units' in the special library area[9] appears to be the derivation of an erroneous assumption, repeated throughout the literature on one-person libraries, that 'there is research which demonstrates that approximately one-third to one-half of all librarians work alone'.[10]

2.4 Estimating the number of solo librarians

The sad tale of the statistician who drowned in the river – average depth one metre – is an apt warning for those who seek to calculate the number of solo librarians.

Certainly there are some one-person or one-professional units in every sector of the profession. School libraries are almost exclusively managed by solo librarians; similarly the first survey of all 119 sixth-form college libraries revealed average staffing of 1.5.[11] Typically National Health Service Librarians work alone, or with minimal clerical support. Together these services give a minimum figure of c.1750.

Experience shows that many special libraries are managed single-handed, or with little help. If the pattern of roughly 50% of industrial, commercial and government libraries being operated by one person has held true since the last DES Census, at least 2300 librarians might be expected to be working solo in the special library sector – but this is mere conjecture.

It is simply not possible to give a comprehensive figure for the number of 'one-man bands'. Nevertheless it seems reasonable to suppose that there are between 1750 and 3900 solo librarians concealed within THE L.I.S.T. and that the actual figure may be considerably higher, allowing for the staff of specialized units not yet included in any official statistics.

One fact is plain: solo information specialists can count on the fact that they are not alone!

References

1 EUCLID, *Feasibility study for an industry training organisation for information and library services: a report by EUCLID to the Information and Library Services Lead Body*, November 1993. Unpublished.
2 Ibid.
3 Library and Information Statistics Unit, Loughborough University, *THE L.I.S.T.: library and information statistics tables for the United Kingdom*, LISU/BLR&DD, 1994.
4 Berridge, P. J. and Sumsion, J., *UK special library statistics: the final report on research commissioned by British Library Research and Development Department*, LISU, August 1994.
5 Serjean, R., *Librarianship and information work: job characteristics and staffing needs*, British Library, 1977.
6 Berridge and Sumsion, op. cit.
7 Serjean, op. cit.
8 East, H., 'Changes in the staffing of UK special libraries and information services in the decade 1972–1981: a review of the DES Census data', *Journal of documentation*, **39** (4), December 1983, 247–65.
9 Ibid.
10 St Clair, G., 'The one-person library: an essay on essentials revisited', *Special libraries*, **78** (4), Fall 1987, 263–70.
11 *Library Association record*, **96** (1), November 1994, 590.

3 The invisible college

Happily no man is an island, not even a 'one-man band'! Each one of us belongs to an 'invisible college', a personal network of people upon whom we can call for information and ideas. The term derives from the academic world, describing the network of researchers in a specific field who maintain close links – through reading, criticizing, debating, perhaps visiting one another, or communicating across the world without ever meeting.

Isolation from other 'Librarylanders' is the price of professional independence, and remains a constant concern for information specialists working alone. Solo information managers need to communicate with peers who share similar challenges, have some appreciation of the workload, can recognize achievements, and can help each other to keep up to date. Moreover it can be a pleasure to speak one's own professional jargon, without having to translate into the 'speak' of colleagues from other professions, or produce concise explanations based on first principles.

Consequently solo librarians and information workers are wise to value links with other information specialists and to maximize the benefits of formal networks with which they are involved. By actively developing the 'college', solo professionals can create a personal support, updating and training structure, through which they can learn from the experience of others and enhance their professional practice.

3.1 Networking

Networking is the normal means by which most people first obtain information, most of the time. It is now a familiar theme in the professional literature, yet its discussion may make the concept seem far removed from a list of telephone numbers pinned on the noticeboard or the folder of 'blurb' collected from other information services, companies, suppliers, professional bodies, training agencies and so on. Nevertheless, together these represent the network of people and organizations able to supply information relevant to the work, and personal development, of the solo librarian and information scientist.

The profession is particularly blessed by the amount of 'free-floating goodwill' (to quote a contributor to the first issue of *OMB newsletter*).[1] This is the basis of the individual's professional information network and must be respected and reciprocated accordingly, not least because the one-person librarian is unable to function effectively without it.

Whether the driving force is a personal desire to enhance skills and deepen understanding, or whether the search is imposed by the demands of 'the job', the information worker needs to tap into the experience and knowledge of others. To quote Segerman-Peck (1991), 'networking is a career tool not to be ignored'.[2]

3.2 Informal networks

Consciously or not, each one of us belongs to interpersonal networks. Note the use of the plural, for every solo professional will certainly be a part of more than one.

3.2.1 *A personal network*

To review the extent of your 'invisible college', begin by identifying your immediate professional network. Consider all the contacts established within the organization. Who are the natural 'gatekeepers' so vital to keeping informed of the latest developments? Next reflect upon one or two recent enquiries which led to an approach to external contacts. List all the people and organizations who might have been contacted to obtain this same information, as well as the ones that were actually used. Appendix 1 illustrates this type of information network. The example shows the framework of services and sources commonly available to health educators in Britain.

In practice, individuals call upon an even wider 'college' to support personal development, knitting together the strands of experience at different times and in different places. The solo practitioner faced with a 'learning problem', or simply the need for information, must think widely. What of former colleagues, fellow students? Think too of contacts in other walks of life whom you respect for their skills and knowledge.

Ask yourself, who do I know:

- who has access to relevant resources?
- who has already done this?
- who knows something about it?
- who may know someone else who knows about this, or who has relevant experience?

One word of caution: remember that those people who are not 'in the business' of providing information are able to assist simply as a spin-off from their primary role. It is especially important not to abuse these sources.

This review will reveal the richness of the network unconsciously constructed in the process of living, studying and working. It should be a source of confidence to the solo professional. Even when you cannot meet your client's information needs, or your personal development needs, you do 'know a man who can'.

3.2.2 *The 'Old Boy' network?*

This term is used advisedly because there is plenty of evidence that young professionals are hesitant to use their connections,[3] and that family commitments hamper the ability of women to develop extensive professional networks.[4] Also it appears that although women are adept at networking to meet the needs of family and friends, they do not automatically transfer this skill to the workplace in support of their own career development.[5]

However, sharing information is the lifeblood of professional practice for the information worker, therefore it is essential to become comfortable and expert at handling personal networks. Far from being manipulative, networks offer a commonsense strategy for 'getting the job done', and for seeking advice, practical help, cooperation and collaboration on matters professional and personal.

Obviously no-one should be in the business of 'cultivating people' because of what they might be able to do for them. In any case interpersonal networks only remain open channels of communication if everyone accepts a responsibility to assist others. Nemeyer (1989) urges the individual to be 'as generous with his or her specific subject specialities and professional time as he or she expects others to be'.[6] Hamilton shows that provided 'we are clear about our motives, and sincere in our respect for the other person', networks are not at all exploitative.[7]

Generally networks emerge naturally, for example through regular use of another information service. However networks can be built, and it is imperative that they are nurtured.

3.2.3 Building informal networks

For the librarian and information worker a review of personal networks always brings to mind services to visit, other specialists to contact, and probably a few people to whom thanks are owed.

Take time to plan how these contacts can be made. In some cases a telephone call to say 'I am here; my service exists, and by the way, what is your operation all about?' will be sufficient. Building up networks is almost certainly a question of mid-term to long-term planning, but its organization is a short-term task not to be deferred. Set priorities, plan a programme of calls and visits over six months or a year, and commit the time ahead in the 'office' diary.

Self-evidently interpersonal skills are of paramount importance in developing interpersonal networks. When planning a visit, it is wise to telephone ahead (or be prepared for the same kind of welcome as the average 'rep' receives). Think kindly of people who come to visit the information unit – networks work both ways. Alan Armstrong has pointed out that suppliers of all kinds work best for those they know best.[8]

On a first visit it is helpful to take some kind of 'gift' bearing your telephone, fax and e-mail numbers, plus a library guide. Prepare a short list of journals, or other resources, to which some kind of access could be allowed. Where staff are likely to be strictly timetabled there can be advantages in booking an appointment around coffee time or even, as the acquaintance progresses, over lunch. Indeed it is possible, in time, to become an honorary affiliate of a much larger service, so that the solo librarian will be invited along to demonstrations, exhibitions and even the pub quiz or Christmas jamboree. The 'official' Christmas card offers a convenient means to thank people for their cooperation during the year.

3.2.4 Starting a new post

Information professionals are well advised to identify those networks that come with the specialism in which they are newly employed straight away. Don't hesitate to telephone around to update whatever kind of 'library' telephone directory has been inherited.

Time spent on introductions around this wider network is an investment which should not be delayed, for without resort to an array of external information sources, it is unlikely that the solo practitioner will be able to function effectively or efficiently in post, let alone lay down a firm platform for personal development. In these early days solo librarians and information managers are in a good position to persuade their management of the importance of allowing time to make contacts, as part of (if not in lieu of) induction training. In any case it is wise to put training and development needs on the agenda at the outset, emphasizing the benefits to the organization of good personal contacts. (See section 7.2.2.)

3.2.5   *Formalizing informal networks: CHIPs*

Occasionally solo information workers, who are already in regular contact, are able to cooperate to extend their connections via jointly organized meetings. This can be a very cost-effective way of developing links with specialist services on whom you may need to call from time to time, and it is not difficult to achieve within a well-defined locality.

One example of such a mutual support network grew from informal liaison between the District Medical Librarian and the Health Education/ Information Officer employed by Croydon Health Authority. CHIPs (Croydon Health Information Providers) operates primarily by telephone, with the help of a straightforward directory. See Appendix 2.

Presently staff from nine separate services participate; one operates a strictly one-person unit, while three manage 'one-professional' services. Meetings, timed around lunch to make it easier for people to attend, are held roughly twice a year. Each meeting allows participants to visit one of the services represented. Meetings follow a fairly standard pattern: each person gives an update on their service, sharing information and concerns. Sometimes guest speakers attend. Otherwise meetings are characterized by the absence of committee papers and the presence of coffee and cakes.

CHIPs has proven to be a useful forum for self-development, enabling discussion of individual experiences and the assessment and comparison of training events, new equipment, recent publications and so on. It is a low-key venture based on a willingness to cooperate, which offers a safe environment in which people can 'fly kites', warn of the coming of 'Barbarians', admit a lack of knowledge and skills, and seek assistance.

The solo information manager, keen to widen the network and include other services within easy reach, may save time and gain more benefit by inviting everyone else to meet on a visit to the unit.

3.3   Formal networks

The efforts of those innovators who set up formal networks from which today's information professionals benefit are often forgotten. Nonetheless, solo librarians are fortunate that so many cooperative networks provide opportunities for continuing education, just as their employers are fortunate that such organizations facilitate access to materials and services.

3.3.1   *Regional networks: BBi and SWTRLS*

Solo workers will be aware of those geographical networks that operate in their 'neck of the woods'. Roaf has demonstrated the benefits and 'trade-offs' inherent in local cooperative schemes.[9]

Two British examples are given here: BBi (Beds & Bucks Information) and SWTRLS (South West Thames Regional Library Service). Both engage in activities of great relevance to librarians working in isolation from their peers.

BBi has seven sector groups covering: business and industry, education, environment, health, local history, marketing and training. The groups aim to develop personal contacts and promote networking, and organize many different training events in a year (exhibitions, courses, seminars, visits and workshadowing as well as more routine meetings). It is BBi policy, as a whole, to hold members' journal listings and the commercial sector find this particularly valuable. Membership fees are reasonable. The network employs a part-time manager and overall development is steered by a business plan, based upon a SWOT analysis.

Within the National Health Service solo librarians and information workers are particularly well served, as the concept of Regional Library Services is highly developed and cooperative initiatives are encouraged. In most regions the challenges of isolation are largely overcome by access to an impressive range of support mechanisms. South West Thames Region is a particularly good example of this, as attested by its quality assurance management manual.[10]

Reviewing the benefits of multitype networks operating in America, Segal emphasizes that network participation 'presents an invaluable method for maintaining and updating one's professional competencies'.[11]

3.3.2 Specialist networks

Few information workers have no-one else with whom they can liaise within their specialized field, although many have to face up to the challenges of overcoming physical isolation from one another.

There is a wide range of groups, independent of the professional bodies: AIMTS (Association for Information Management and Technology Staff in the NHS), CSL (Circle of State Librarians), FIG (Fire Information Group – UK) and WILG (Water Industry Librarians Group) to name just four. A few special groups, like the Independent Schools Librarians' Group for East Anglia, also have a regional focus.

Dale's *Directory* is the best guide to groups in the United Kingdom.[12] BLISS (The British Library Information Sciences Service) can provide details of relevant organizations, while the professional bodies will give information about their own specialized groupings.

3.4 The contribution of professional bodies

Professional bodies are a real blessing to the lone librarian, albeit one which can hit the pay packet quite hard! Happily a subscription to a professional body pays dividends even for those who choose just 'to stand and stare', for the publications (articles, reports, news, notices of continuing education programmes, book reviews, trade literature and so on) all help to keep one up to date.

3.4.1 The library and information sector

Although many librarians and information scientists maintain dual membership, it is almost inevitable that 'Librarylanders' should develop a kind of 'brand loyalty' to one of the Big Three (Aslib, the Institute of Information Scientists and The Library Association) and, either by cause or effect, to one of its special-interest groups. Undoubtedly individuals are influenced by established personal contacts, and by the level of camaraderie achieved by different groups.

The pioneering work of Aslib's 'One-Man Band Group' must be recognized. OMB is a boon for those whose organizations are corporate members. Individuals may affiliate to the group independently, although the relatively small size of this network suggests that membership of Aslib is perceived as a barrier. Not so! Convincing management of the value of corporate membership might be an interesting test of powers of persuasion.

Each of the professional associations hosts a range of groups and branches. Within The Library Association, the Industrial and Commercial Libraries Group has demonstrated a particular awareness of the needs of lone operators among its membership. The Health Libraries Group targets 'one man' bands and also welcomes members who do not belong to The LA. The advent of the Special Libraries Committee may also give solo librarians a higher profile within The LA. Other groups, for instance the School Libraries Group, comprise a majority of members who work on their own or in one-professional libraries.

School librarians also benefit from the active publishing and training programme of the School Library Association. All four professional bodies are listed in Appendix 3.

3.4.2 *Other professional bodies*

Many solo information workers find it at least expedient, and at best valuable, to pursue membership of a professional body in the field in which they work. Webb's study of best practice[13] across the range of professional firms demonstrates the considerable diversity of memberships held by library and information personnel working in special libraries.

3.5 Playing an active part

There is a responsibility for information professionals to participate, in some measure, in those networks which prove to be a vital resource in meeting the information needs of their employers. However, it can be difficult to decide which organizations to join, which to stay with, and in which to become more involved.

The solo worker has to make judgments about costs and benefits. Don't be afraid to try out different groups. Generally when membership has ceased to be either a pleasure, or of personal value, it is time to look elsewhere for support and opportunities to develop. Managers of one-person units may find that, in practice, it is easier to argue the case for participation at the 'firm's' time and expense if they have already taken on some kind of committee function. Burge (1992) emphasizes committee work as a 'very useful way to develop a network, to meet people, and learn the skills of committee work and presentation'.[14] St Clair and Williamson (1992) write of the librarian's obligation to discuss openly the advantages for the employer of active participation in professional activities.[15]

Nevertheless it may be entirely unrealistic to consider playing an active part just now. In this, as in every other aspect of working as the sole information professional within a unit, good time management is vital. The individual's choice needs to reflect the value of time at work as well as any pressures on leisure time. Fortunately, some of the benefits of membership remain whatever the decision.

3.6 Colleagues

Many solo librarians work among professionals who bear great responsibilities for providing accurate information: doctors, engineers, lawyers, pharmacists, sales representatives and teachers among them. Confident of their own expertise, information professionals do well to recognize that colleagues and clients from other disciplines have knowledge, skills and experience from which to learn.

While the solo information worker may sometimes feel an outsider amidst the jargon and humour of another profession, it is wise to embrace the contribution that new insights make to personal development, and to welcome colleagues into the 'invisible college'.

3.7 A caveat

St Clair (1989) rightly argues that interpersonal networking is 'the key to excellence'.[16] Nevertheless it is not a 'cure-all'. Reynolds (1980) warns that cooperation cannot 'nullify the consequences of fundamental deficiencies and constraints', and this is especially pertinent to the single-handed library manager.[17] While nurturing networks on the one hand, the solo librarian must also look to agreeing realistic objectives, establishing a satisfactory level of professional service, and developing personal competencies on the other!

References

1 West, L. E., Letter published in *OMB newsletter*, No. 1, Sept. 1982.
2 Segerman-Peck, L., *Networking and mentoring: a woman's guide*, Piatkus, 1991.
3 Hamilton, R., *Mentoring: a practical guide to the skills of mentoring*, The Industrial Society, 1993.
4 Willis, L. and Daisley, J., *Developing women through training: a practical handbook*, McGraw-Hill, 1992.
5 Segerman-Peck, op. cit.
6 Nemeyer, C., quoted by St Clair, G., 'Interpersonal networking: it is who you know', *Special libraries*, **80** (2), Spring 1989, 107–12.
7 Hamilton, op. cit.
8 Armstrong, A., Letter published in *OMB newsletter*, No. 23, Spring 1988.
9 Roaf, M., 'The industrial library and the information network', *Information and library manager*, **4** (2), 1984, 47–9.
10 South West Thames Regional Library Service, *A quality library service: management manual for healthcare libraries*, SWTRLS, 1993.
11 Segal, J. S., 'Special libraries and multitype networks', *Special libraries*, **80** (2), Spring 1989, 85–93.
12 Dale, P., *Directory of library and information organizations in the United Kingdom*, Library Association Publishing, 1993.
13 Webb, S. P., *Best practice?: continuing professional development for library/information staff in UK professional firms*, British Library R&D Report: no. 6039, Webb, 1991.
14 Burge, S., 'Professional development of librarians in the Civil Service', in Foreman, L. (ed.), *Developing professionals in information work: personal and organizational growth in libraries*, Circle of State Librarians, 1992.
15 St Clair, G. and Williamson, J., *Managing the new one-person library*, 2nd edn, Bowker-Saur, 1992.
16 St Clair (1989), op. cit.
17 Reynolds, M. M., 'Library cooperation: the ideal and the reality'. Reprinted in Layzell Ward, P. (ed.), *The professional development of the librarian and information worker*, Aslib, 1980, 158–65.

The development needs of solo information workers

'Single-handed' librarians and information scientists are employed at the frontiers of professional practice. Brindley (1987) has predicted opportunities for 'new forms of information-related work in entrepreneurial settings, as information broker or consultant and more frequently as "one-man bands"', heralding an age 'both of the professional polymath and the professional specialist'.[1]

A detailed picture of the skills needed by solo information workers can be drawn. However, it is essential that individuals give due weight to the shortcomings of the information profession in general, as perceived by employers. Also it is helpful for isolated information workers to see their own needs in the context of the demand for continuing professional development from the wider profession.

4.1 The broadening role of information managers

As the 'moving front' of the information industry advances (see section 2.1)[2] those information workers forging new paths for the profession face new challenges. The broadening role of the library and information science practitioner is not restricted to applications of information management within the employing organization, or to the application of information technology. Webb's study of professional associations and private professional practices[3] (in accountancy, law and so on) showed significant involvement in marketing, public relations and training, although there was no common profile. Indeed the placing of library services within the organizational structure actually reflects the changing roles of information professionals: almost half formed part of another department, for example computer services, consultancy, marketing or research.

The Library Association's Futures Working Party highlighted the wide range of jobs in which information professionals work, identifying some 60 information handling occupations including advice centre manager, database coordinator, information engineer and publications officer.[4]

New responsibilities and challenges give even greater significance to the individual's ability to define and meet personal needs for continuing professional development.

4.2 Meeting the needs of employers

Some solo professionals will feel unable to share Burrington's confidence that 'librarians will become even more necessary',[5] in the light of Moore's discovery that information graduates win fewer than half the posts specifically advertised to them.[6]

4.2.1 *Portable skills*

Gash and Reardon's study (1988) of personal transferable skills highlighted some of the issues of concern to employers.[7] Obviously core communication skills (embracing oral, written and interpersonal skills, including working with groups) are required for the role of information intermediary within a team. They are also as basic to the armoury of skills which must be carried into new, more active roles in exploiting information, as traditional skills in librarianship and information work.

Communication skills dominate the list of requirements of employers as expressed by the Standing Conference of Employers of Graduates.[8] Usherwood reported that librarians employing new staff similarly 'indicate a high demand for human resource management, interpersonal and communication skills'.[9] However Gash and Reardon reported that, in practice, employers 'are not altogether happy with the level of personal transferable skills displayed by information graduates'.[10]

4.2.2 *The management perspective*

Slater's (1988) study of internal training and external short courses in the 'special library' sector[11] revealed an interesting dichotomy between the perceptions of information staff and those of their immediate managers. Managers placed more emphasis on the need for their information staff to gain wider background knowledge of the context in which they worked: 23% identified skill gaps in this area, compared with only 9% of staff. This mismatch raises the spectre of the 'special librarian' burrowing away, busily engaged in activities which fail to address the agenda of the employing organization!

On the other hand, Collins and Shuter's (1984) survey of 128 isolated professionals found that difficulty in 'knowing what's going on' in the organization is one of the most disappointing aspects of the work of 'one-man bands'.[12] Similarly Roberts's (1979) analysis of questionnaires from 251 'special librarians' found considerable dissatisfaction with the communication of general information 'about what's happening elsewhere in the organization, about future plans, etc.'.[13] In view of the dissatisfaction of employers, the solo information worker needs to take personal responsibility for initiating methods of becoming better informed as to the affairs and activities of the parent organization.

Slater also found that staff placed priority on management skills; perceived as a skill gap by 29%, but only by 8% of their managers.[14] Unfortunately this reflects a common underestimation by employers of the skills required to manage a small specialized information unit. Solo librarians may well identify the education of managers as a long-term mission, remembering that the converted make powerful proponents of the cause.

One of the most worrying findings in Slater's survey is that while 18% of staff recognized the need to acquire further computer skills, a total of 43% of managers cited computing skills as necessary but absent among their information staff.[15] This gap in perception highlights an image prevalent in some circles that librarians are being left behind, as more imaginative professionals seize the opportunities offered by new technology. It reveals how important it is to develop skills in information technology, and also suggests a need to keep abreast of developments in the application of IT elsewhere in the organization.

Solo librarians are perpetually vulnerable to 'downsizing', and ignore such reports of the dissatisfaction of employers at their peril.

4.3 Studies of development needs in mainstream librarianship

The lack of day-to-day contact with fellow information specialists tends to undermine confidence, generating anxiety among solo librarians as to their competence in relation to professionals in the mainstream of practice. Thus it is helpful to set the needs of solo workers in the context of their peers.

In recent years a number of studies have identified perceived needs for professional development, preferred means of addressing these, and monitored the supply and demand for training. Although differences of emphasis have been revealed between different sectors of the profession, and between services of different size, the similarity of the research findings provides compelling evidence.

4.3.1 *Dominant themes*

Demand for activities regarding computer applications and management dominate the training 'market', with a sizeable demand for furthering knowledge and skills in support of serving specific user groups and managing specific collections.

Ritchie (1988) surveyed attitudes towards management development among 1600 members of The Library Association, concentrating on librarians at post-experience level.[16] The responses highlighted four key areas in which training was needed to meet current responsibilities: computing, management, librarianship and information skills, followed by specialized subject knowledge.

The research by MacDougall, Lewins and Tseng (1990)[17] showed considerable similarity between the expressed needs reported by Ritchie, and the continuing education actually pursued by librarians and information staff within British academic, public and school libraries. In the course of one year (1987/8) almost half of respondents participated in some kind of activity on different aspects of librarianship and information work (including the needs of special user groups such as children and young people, and collection management). One quarter had experienced training in management, and one in five had pursued activities regarding information technology.

The Bombay study by Jani, Parekh and Sen (1991)[18] (in which 27.5% of respondents managed one-professional units) also echoed Ritchie's findings. The most popular subjects for professional development activities had been: reference and information work, computers and information technology, management and library skills. A need for additional technology-oriented knowledge and skills in future was expressed by 75% of respondents and almost half wished to pursue management training, including public relations, communication skills and interpersonal skills.

4.3.2 *Interpersonal skills*

Levy and Usherwood's (1992) research demonstrated the need for staff to be competent and confident in conducting work relationships, yet noted that the 'people dimension' is often neglected.[19] They have developed a conceptual model 'which is a powerful illustration of the variety and complexity of the interpersonal dimension of library work'.[20] See Appendix 4.

4.3.3 *Specific needs of women*

A recent survey of women's training needs by the Industrial Society[21] identified priorities in the following areas: management, understanding finance, interpersonal skills including presentation skills, self-management, information technology and career development. The need for women to improve their networking skills has also been demonstrated (see section 3.2.2).

4.4 School libraries

Evidence from the American Association of School Librarians,[22] which conducted a survey in 1987, showed that school librarians place priority on the application of microcomputers and online searching skills. In addition they call for more continuing education activities on designing instruction on information skills and on evaluating programme performance.

4.5 'Special libraries'

Broadbent and Grosser's (1987) study of Australian special libraries and information centres[23] demonstrated that their staff share the same need to continue professional development regarding management and new technology as colleagues in other sectors. Highest priority was given to information technology (specifically online searching, microcomputers and automated systems) and planning. When asked to establish priorities for future development, database design was added to the list. Just over 15% of the information professionals in this survey managed one-person units.

Of Slater's sample of the British 'Special' sector[24] 29% managed one-professional units (with no more than one assistant); another 10% were strictly one-person librarians. Across the whole sample, skill and aptitude gaps were again experienced in computing, management and interpersonal areas (including user relations and communicative, presentational and instructive skills).

4.6 Williamson's study of one-person units

In 1987 Williamson[25] surveyed the staff of 82 one-person libraries and information units, comprising members of Aslib's 'One-Man Band' group plus members of INVOG (an information network which was coordinated by the National Council of Voluntary Organizations). The study included six case studies and an extensive literature review of the education and training needs of solo information workers.

Williamson's research showed that one-person librarians share the same broad needs for training and further development as the rest of the profession. Respondents to the questionnaire placed priority upon the following:[26]

- new technology
- information sources
- evaluation of user needs
- information retrieval
- communications skills
- personal development

The study also illustrated the importance of factors which distinguish the role of solo information professionals from peers employed in the mainstream, notably greater needs for interpersonal networking, self-motivation, self-management and subject specialization, accompanied by high levels of interpersonal skills.

4.7 The development needs of solo information professionals

Drawing upon the views of employers, research in all sectors of library and information work, studies of 'one-person' units, the literature of solo librarianship, plus evidence of the skills required by managers in all disciplines, a clear picture of areas in which one-person and one-professional librarians may need to gain knowledge, and develop or enhance skills, appears.

4.7.1 A checklist

This checklist offers a framework within which solo librarians and information workers may consider their personal need to gain further knowledge, enhance skills and review attitudes:

- organizational culture
- management
- interpersonal skills
- communication
- information technology
- library and information skills
- networking
- subject knowledge
- personal development

4.7.2 Organizational culture

One-person operators need to understand the purpose and culture of the organization within which they are working, so that they can define the value which the information service can add to the parent institution, establish the role and policy of the information unit, offer appropriate services to users, and prioritize conflicting demands upon time and other resources.

Brindley (1987) emphasizes the need for political skills of persuasion and presentation.[27] These call for a sound understanding of where power lies within the organization, recognizing who has influence, who has authority and who is decisive.

On a day-to-day level, the solo librarian must observe quickly, and then decide how far to conform to the organization's code of dress, style of meetings and conduct of relationships in the workplace. Induction training, or its absence, will give some indication of organizational culture, but this will certainly require further investigation and reflection.

4.7.3 Management

Williamson (1991) highlighted the pressure on one-person librarians to exercise 'many more management skills earlier in their careers than their contemporaries'.[28] The call for a wide array of management skills runs, as a common thread, through the literature of the field.

Based on experience in facilitating managers to identify their own learning needs, Roobottom has developed a model of skills[29] which may need to be developed to improve management performance in specific areas. This model can usefully be adapted and applied to the management role of the solo information professional as follows:

Area	Skills/knowledge
Task management	Analysis of user needs
	Establishing service aims and objectives
	Prioritizing
	Planning and organizing
	Innovation
	Time management
	Quality management
	Delegation
Self-management	Self-analysis
	Self-motivation
	Setting aims and objectives
	Time-management
	Stress management
	Awareness of learning styles
	Networking
Career management	Awareness of values
	Awareness of personality
	Setting personal goals
	Visibility: impact presentation
	Use of mentor

The model itself reinforces the importance of the interrelated skills of time-management, goal-setting and planning, the need for which dominates the day-to-day experience, and the writings, of one-person operators.

All these areas of management are underpinned by competent decision-making and the ability to manage change effectively since change is the norm for the one-person practitioner. Roberts (1979) found that change is viewed in a positive light, and intimates that 'special librarians' are distinguished by their 'greater willingness to adapt to what may be called information circumstances'.[30]

Single-handed information staff may also need to develop skills in certain specific management techniques, so as to run units effectively and efficiently, for example financial management (to include strategies for competing for financial resources and perhaps active fundraising) and the use of statistics.

Chapter 9 looks further at the question of career development. Meanwhile people management is of such importance to the work of the solo information manager that it is given separate consideration below.

4.7.4　Interpersonal skills

Applying Roobottom's (1988) model,[31] solo workers need to ensure that they are skilled in the following areas:

People management	Assertiveness
	Listening
	Giving and receiving feedback
	Challenging
	Negotiation
	Leadership
	Working with groups:
	• meetings
	• teamwork
	• training
	Self-awareness
	• personality
	• personal style

Achieving skills in assertiveness is a priority for solo librarians and information workers. Assertiveness training 'provides individuals with a convenient handle by which to examine their own habitual responses to certain situations; to bolster low self-esteem and seek to communicate more assertively at work'.[32]

Levy and Usherwood's (1992) model of interpersonal skills[33] is helpful to individuals seeking to identify personal development needs in this crucial area. See Appendix 4.

One of the more demanding aspects of the role of the solo information worker is that, since colleagues are potential clients, it is generally inappropriate to share exasperations and frustrations within the workplace. The lone librarian has always 'got to accentuate the positive, eliminate the negative, latch on to the affirmative, and don't mess with Mister in between'![34]

4.7.5 *Communication*

The success of any small information service depends upon its ability to market the service, matching 'your capabilities with the needs of your customers, so that they respond by taking action profitable to you'.[35]

All communications from the one-person unit (from the response to an enquiry to the annual report) should be seen as a form of marketing; a means of promoting the range of services to targeted groups to meet the needs of the organization. As one contributor to *OMB newsletter* pointed out, 'The solo information provider cannot afford to blush unseen or be sadly missed after receiving a P45. Your value to the organization has to be visible . . .'[36]

Solo librarians may require competence in many forms of oral and written communication: public speaking, report writing, desktop publishing, editing, displays and press work, to name a few. Investment in developing these communication skills, plus the interpersonal skills discussed above, equip the information specialist with those portable skills in such demand from employers. See section 4.2 above.

4.7.6 *Information technology*

Brindley (1987) argues that information technology skills are of 'pivotal importance'; 'a prerequisite' for managerial credibility.[37] Jago has confirmed that for librarians entering the employment market, ability in exploiting information technology is the most marketable skill of all.[38]

Solo staff often find themselves at the end of the spectrum: either hard-pushed to get access to a photocopier or almost submerged in IT. Each position presents challenges for personal development. Appropriate use of information technology transforms routine library administration, brings dramatic improvements to the presentation of information to users, and enhances the quality of the service. To achieve such gains, the information manager will need knowledge and skills, and be able to reach decisions on hardware and software relevant to several operations, ranging from budgeting to database creation.

Reflecting the experience of information workers in all sectors, respondents to Williamson's survey[39] cited information services, information retrieval and new technology as training priorities. Certainly the benefits of using computerized systems within the information service are obvious although Williamson has warned that one 'should think very carefully about why a computer is needed, and what cost-benefits will result'.[40]

Not surprisingly, users place considerable value on database searching. Research by Matarazzo, Prusak and Gauthier[41] showed that users of Corporate Libraries in the States placed the highest value on this service.

4.7.7   *Library and information skills*

No amount of new technology will obviate the need for the efficient practice of basic library skills: acquisition, organization of resources (often according to specialized classification schemes), disseminating information, loan systems, interlibrary cooperation and user education; all aimed at providing a response to enquiries, and at meeting and anticipating information needs.

The one-person unit must focus services on the current and future needs of users, and respond quickly to shifting emphases within the employing organization. This explains the priority which one-person librarians attach to skills in evaluating services and conducting user surveys.

4.7.8   *Networking*

Padden (1986) comments that the solitary librarian 'experiences two forms of isolation: she is isolated within her environment, and from her own professional colleagues'.[42] Moreover Brindley notes that 'a good informal network of backup contacts will be required for survival and success'.[43] See Chapter 3.

4.7.9   *Subject knowledge*

The centrality of subject knowledge and skills to the work of solo information professionals accords subject specialization a high priority as a development need. Inevitably, highly individualized approaches may be required to remedy these gaps.

The drive to develop expertise outside librarianship and information science, for instance in commercial subjects, is a consequence of the broadening role of information professionals which has been noted in research in Australia and Denmark, as well as Britain.[44]

4.7.10 *Personal development*

To quote Brindley (1987), 'How easily all these needs can be expressed – how large a challenge to put all this into practice.'[45]

The demand for opportunities for personal development from the 'one-person librarians' surveyed by both Collins and Shuter (1984),[46] and Williamson (1988),[47] is significant. In the first place it appears to reflect some frustration with the opportunities for career development in one-person and one-professional libraries. This issue is explored further in Chapter 9. Secondly, it suggests recognition of the influence of personal characteristics and of interpersonal skills on the effectiveness of the single-handed library manager. Finally it also appears to reflect the importance of the relationship between personal development and motivation. For this reason Chapter 5 is devoted to the subject of self-motivation.

References

1 Brindley, L., 'Management development for information professionals of the future', *Aslib proceedings*, **39** (9), 1987, 235–43.

2 EUCLID, *Feasibility study for an industry training organisation for information and and library services: a report by EUCLID to the Information and Library Services Lead Body*, November 1993. Unpublished.

3 Webb, S. P., *Best practice?: continuing professional development for library/information staff in UK professional firms*, British Library R&D Report: no. 6039, Webb, 1991.

4 Gash, S. and Reardon, D. F., 'Personal transferable skills for the modern information professional: a discussion paper', *Journal of information science*, **14**, 1988, 285–92.

5 Burrington, G., 'From here to eternity', *Library Association record*, **96** (11), November 1994, 617–18.

6 Moore, N., *The emerging markets for librarians and information workers*, British Library, 1987. Library and Information Research Report 56.

7 Gash and Reardon, op. cit.

8 Ibid.

9 Foreman, L. (ed.), *Developing professionals in information work: personal and organizational growth in libraries*, Circle of State Librarians, 1992.

10 Gash and Reardon, op. cit.

11 Slater, M., *Internal training and external short courses: a study of informal continuing education in the special library/information field*, British Library Research Paper 52, 1988.

12 Shuter, J., 'The isolated professional', *Information and library manager*, **3** (4), 1984, 106–13.

13 Roberts, N., 'Special librarians: job characteristics and work attitudes', *Journal of librarianship*, **11** (1), January 1979, 4–14.

14 Slater, op. cit.

15 Ibid.

16 Ritchie, S., *Training and management development in librarianship*, British Library, 1988. Library and Information Research Report 34.

17 MacDougall, J., Lewins, H. and Tseng, G., *Continuing education and training opportunities in librarianship: a study of participation, benefits and defects*, British Library Research & Development Department, 1990. British Library Research Paper 74.

18 Jani, N., Parekh, H. and Sen, B., 'Individual perceptions of professional advancement', *Libri*, **41** (3), 1991, 183–93.

19 Levy, P. and Usherwood, B., *People skills: interpersonal skills training for library and information work*, British Library, 1992. Library & Information Research Report 88.

20 Levy, P., *Interpersonal skills*, Library Association Publishing, 1993.

21 Morris, B., *Training and development for women*, Library Association Publishing, 1993.

22 Mancall, J. C. and Bertland, L. H., 'Step one reported: analysis of AASL's first needs assessment for continuing education', *School library media quarterly*, **16** (2), Winter 1988, 88–98.

23 Broadbent, M. and Grosser, K., 'Continuing professional development of Special Library and Information Center managers', *Journal of education for library and information science*, **28** (2), Fall 1987, 99–115.

24 Slater, op. cit.

25 Williamson, J., 'One person libraries and information units: their education and training needs', *Library management*, **9** (5), MCB Press, 1988.

26 Ibid.

27 Brindley, op. cit.

28 Williamson, J., 'One person libraries and information units: their education and training needs', *Library and information research news*, **14** (5), Summer 1991, 12–19.

29 Roobottom, C. and Winkles, T., 'Self-appraisal – a route to self-development', in Pedler, M., Burgoyne, J. and Boydell, T. (eds.), *Applying self-development in organizations*, Prentice-Hall, 1988.

30 Roberts, op. cit.

31 Roobottom and Winkles, op. cit.

32 Lacey Bryant, S., 'A woman not in libraries', *New library world*, August 1991, 6–9.

33 Levy and Usherwood, op. cit.

34 Crosby, B., 'Accentuate the positive', popular song. Source: audiocassette *Best of Bing Crosby*, Oct. 1987, TC MFP 5814.

35 Wood, D., 'Improving your image: how to promote a library or information service', *Aslib proceedings*, **36** (10), October 1984.

36 Beasley, E., in *OMB newsletter*, 36 Summer 1991.

37 Brindley, op. cit.

38 Foreman, op. cit.

39 Williamson, *Library management*, op. cit.

40 Quoted by Harris, S., in *OMB newsletter*, 29 Autumn 1989.

41 St Clair, G. and Williamson, J., *Managing the new one-person library*, 2nd edn, Bowker-Saur, 1992.

42 Padden, S., 'The loneliness of the one-woman library', *Wilpower*, **33**, 1986, 9–10.

43 Brindley, op. cit.

44 Casteleyn, M. and Webb, S. P., *Promoting excellence: personnel management and staff development in libraries*, Bowker-Saur, 1993.

45 Brindley, op. cit.

46 Shuter, op. cit.

47 Williamson, *Library management*, op. cit.

5 Self-motivation

It appears that some people are born motivated, some people achieve motivation and some people have motivation thrust upon them! Indeed much of the writing on motivational theory is reminiscent of the 'nature' versus 'nurture' debate on child and personality development.

Although motivation is a complex drive, which arises from the balance between human needs and environmental and occupational factors, it is within the sphere of personal control. For the solo librarian and information worker the ability to initiate developments, and drive them forward to completion, is crucial to the quality of the information service and to personal and professional growth.

5.1 Motivation and the isolated professional

Collins and Shuter (1984)[1] made a brave attempt to study the relationship between performance and job satisfaction among isolated information workers, by applying Herzberg's much criticized psychological theory of motivation in a survey of 128 'one-man bands'.

Although the methodology proved to be flawed, so that their findings were dominated by 'the value-judgements of a self-selected sample',[2] nevertheless the research successfully illuminated the extent to which experience met the expectations of 'OMBs' (the acronym used by the two researchers). From this work it was possible to build up a picture of the 'average' OMB, the 'dissatisfied' OMB and the 'satisfied' OMB.[3]

Shuter reported that all OMBs find the interest of the work they are engaged in, and its variety, come up to their expectations. Satisfied OMBs ranked three other key factors of the job which met expectations: trying out new ideas, being appreciated and job satisfaction.[4]

On the other hand, all OMBs are disappointed with their level of knowledge of what is going on in the organization, with the amount of training, and with their pay. Furthermore, dissatisfied OMBs appear to be demotivated by lack of appreciation and the lack of opportunities for personal development.[5]

Since training and personal development are among the most disappointing aspects of the job for the 'average' OMB, there can be no question of the importance of self-motivation, and of formulating a personal development plan. Honest recognition of your own motivators, and an understanding of how you can boost and maintain motivation, is a vital element of personal development.

5.2 Professional values

Traditionally, librarianship and information science has attracted people who perceive the work as being intrinsically meaningful, socially significant, and an occupation in which the objectives of the individual are compatible with those of the organization.[6]

Despite market-testing in public services, local management in schools and an internal market in the National Health Service, the issues around providing (and obtaining) information in a profit-making and competitive environment have not been fully explored outside the confines of 'special' librarianship, and perhaps not fully within it.

One-person operators have a particular need to explore and confront their own value system. It is self-evident that the individual taking responsibility for an information service in commerce, industry, a non-government organization or a research body, must ensure that the primary goals of the employing organization do not conflict with personal values. Similarly those entering public service in a school or hospital must feel comfortable with the ethos of the service. Otherwise solo workers risk a great disservice to their clients, and a period of misery. Willis and Daisley (1990) point out that 'When your values aren't being met, it gives rise to dissatisfaction, complaints, and niggles, and your energy drains away'.[7]

5.3　Personal values

' . . . to thine own self be true, / And it must follow, as the night the day, Thou canst not then be false to any man.'[8]

Plate and Stone (1980) observed that 'To feel that one has grown depends on achievement in tasks that have meaning to the individual.'[9] Personal excellence, effectiveness and balance, require that we are in touch with our values, which develop, change and may become indistinct with the passage of time!

Raven (1984) shows that recognition of basic values enables individuals to identify and reconcile conflicts which may inhibit performance at work and career development.[10] Longer term, it enables people to consider the likely consequences of pursuing the values to which they are attached, to envisage the type of job (and lifestyle) which would be personally satisfying, and to plan personal and professional development accordingly.

5.3.1　*Identifying personal values*

Spending some time on clarifying personal values is not esoteric, but an important exercise in managing personal motivation and development. The following questions provide a starting point:

- What are your most important personal aims?
  What kind of person do you want to become?
- Picture yourself in 20 years' time. How do you see your life then?
- You discover that you are likely to die within a matter of weeks. Which three things will you most regret not having done?
  When do you plan to do them?
- Name your greatest personal qualities.
- List your greatest professional abilities.
- What are your most important professional goals: This year? In the next three years? Five years? Beyond that?

Trask and Wood (1984) have developed a 'Career Anchor Self-analysis form' for librarians and information workers.[11] Also, it may help to look at some of the guides for people considering a career change which offer detailed exercises for self-analysis. See the section on career development in the select bibliography.

5.3.2 Prepare a personal profile

Self-knowledge is the most challenging aspect of personal development. It is important to recognize attitudes towards time and achievement, for instance the balance between paid work, other pursuits which you value, your social life and domestic responsibilities. Recognition of personality traits, such as whether you are an introvert or an extrovert, is helpful. Personality tests, like Myers-Briggs[12] and Belbin[13] can be a source of insight. Training units in large organizations usually have access to personality tests.

Compiling a personal profile, which encapsulates these matters of personality and style, values, beliefs and attitudes, provides the foundation of a personal portfolio (see section 6.1). Moreover, it serves as a prelude to formulating a professional development plan.

5.4 Self-management: setting personal goals

The preparation of a personal plan, which is anchored in a sound understanding of personal values and designed to meet realistic and concrete targets, is a powerful agent of professional development. Appendix 5 illustrates one approach to developing a personal strategy for career development.

The aim is to set challenges which will be a pleasure to pursue (for the most part), and the achievement of which will bring personal satisfaction. Hurdles to be overcome to like yourself more, or to impress others, have no place here. It is essential that you will value the accomplishment of the targets you set and that you believe you can achieve them with sufficient effort.

In order to command sufficient commitment to motivate professional development, personal goals should meet certain criteria.[14] Goals must be:

- real   – concrete and specific;
- realistic   – challenging but attainable;
- valued   – based upon personal values;
- measurable   – verifiable in some way;
- recorded   – subject to monitoring, review, and, in due course, self-congratulation.

Odiorne suggests the following aims: use imagination to make your job a different one, develop an area of expertise (either by building on strengths or by consciously acquiring and developing new skills) and learn a challenging new task or skill each year.[15]

Goal-setting is an effective motivational technique, which gives direction to planned professional development.

References

1   Shuter, J., 'The isolated professional', *Information and library manager*, **3** (4), 1984, 106–13.
2   Ibid.
3   Ibid.
4   Ibid.
5   Ibid.
6   Plate, K. H. and Stone, E. W., 'Factors affecting librarians' job satisfac-

tion: a report of two studies'. Reprinted in Layzell Ward, P. (ed.), *The professional development of the librarian and information worker*, Aslib, 1980, 186–99.

7 Willis, L. and Daisley, J., *Springboard: women's development workbook*, Hawthorn Press, 1990.

8 Shakespeare, W., spoken by Polonius, *Hamlet*, **I**. iii. 78.

9 Plate and Stone, op. cit.

10 Raven, J., *Competence in modern society: its identification, development and release*, H. K. Lewis & Co., 1984.

11 Trask, M. and Wood, J., *Career planning and assessment for librarians*, Kuring-gai College of Advanced Education, Lindfield, New South Wales, 1984.

12 Hedges, P., *Understanding your personality with Myers-Briggs and more*, Sheldon Press, 1993.

13 Belbin, R. M., *Management teams: why they succeed or fail*, 2nd edn, Heinemann, 1989.

14 Timm, P. R., *Successful self-management: a sound approach to personal effectiveness*, Kogan Page, 1987.

15 Weihrich, H. and Koontz, H., *Management: a global perspective*, 10th edn, International edn, McGraw-Hill Inc., 1993.

6 A personal plan for professional development

The most important factor in preparing a professional development plan is a sense of self: that your personal development is as deserving of a high standard of planning as the information service for which you are responsible. The importance of self-motivation, as the pivot upon which personal professional development rests, has been discussed in the previous chapter. Two more ingredients are critical to the success of any personal plan: flexibility and creative thinking.

Everyone takes their own approach to planning professional development. The strategy described here is just one model, which may be adapted at will. Nevertheless it incorporates three key steps central to the process: a 'self-audit', the identification of required skills, knowledge and attitudes, and the setting of objectives.

The 'building blocks' upon which the information worker can construct a personal development plan have already been introduced:

'Self-audit'
- Recognition of personal values and aspirations. See Section 5.3.
- Recognition of interests, attitudes and style, attributes and abilities. (Preferably recorded within a personal profile.) See section 5.3.2.

Identification of professional development needs
The analysis of development needs is considered below; the process suggested here draws upon the checklist for solo information workers. See section 4.7.1.

For managers of one-person and one-professional units, analysis of what needs to be learned to improve personal performance and prepare for opportunities ahead, requires a re-examination of the purpose and priorities of the information unit. A review of its role and projected needs, combined with an evaluation of current services, facilitates effective planning of the information service and contributes to the planning of personal professional development.

Once the self-audit has been completed (incorporating long-term aspirations) and gaps and weaknesses in skills and knowledge have been defined, the individual can move on to *setting meaningful goals* and devising a workable plan to achieve them.

The process itself is of value; it serves to dispel any notion that solo librarians and information workers are 'hostages to fortune'. By acknowledging personal interests and aspirations, and assessing the influences upon the environment within which they work, and upon the wider profession, it becomes evident that much can be anticipated. There is much to be gained by developing those professional skills which are likely to be needed in future – either to grasp opportunities which may arise or to face challenges which lie ahead.

6.1 A written plan

In the past, very few information workers, including those who have given serious thought to personal, professional and career development, actually went so far as to commit their plans for personal professional development to paper.

With the introduction of The Library Association's Framework for Continuing Professional Development this situation has begun to change. Love it or loathe it, *Your personal profile,*[1] a workbook which is an integral part of the framework, gives food for thought. Its systematic approach to personal development is outlined in the 'Guidelines for individuals'. See Appendix 6.

Admittedly there is no absolute need to record what you plan to achieve, but Timm argues that an unrecorded goal is only a wish![2] Planning professional development without making any effort to record its goals (on paper, or disk or by confiding in someone whom you respect) is rather like 'Believing without belonging';[3] it smacks of lack of commitment.

6.2 Develop a personal portfolio

In recent years much interest has been shown in portfolio-based learning, in which a personal portfolio is prepared to aid and document personal professional development.

Redman (1994) sees the personal portfolio as 'a means of gaining a more positive self-image. It helps people to know what they have to offer . . . It will also give them a greater ability to take control of their future.'[4] Redman's account of the steps involved in compiling a portfolio of prior learning experiences to develop a learning programme is a useful tool for individual portfolio development.

Under the regulations governing admission to the Register as an Associate of The Library Association, introduced in 1995, candidates may opt to submit a portfolio of evidence of professional development (see section 8.2).

6.3 Enlist the help of others

Germain believes that 'approximately 5% of the population are capable of developing themselves. The other 95% need help from other people.'[5] This highlights the valuable role of mentors (see section 7.4.5).

In fact much can be achieved alone and several different ways of analysing personal training needs are discussed below. Feedback on individual performance is essential; the management perspective is most important. Many solo information workers are employed in sectors with well-established procedures for staff appraisal, so that opportunities to consider personal performance, discuss personal achievements and 'flag up' areas of concern will arise naturally.

Those who do not benefit from regular performance reviews are wise to initiate such an opprtunity, by making an appointment with the appropriate person (perhaps the line manager or head of department). One way or another, it is important to approach people who can assist in identifying present development needs, and assessing future areas for professional development.

6.4 Needs analysis

Taking the time to identify those areas in which new or enhanced expertise is required allows the preparation of a proactive personal plan, which directs professional development, rather than merely reacting to needs and opportunities on an *ad hoc* basis.

There is a wealth of material on which to draw in analysing areas of professional practice which could be improved and in anticipating other areas for personal development. The most valuable resource at your disposal is honesty. Remember that 'in self-definition of capacities and qualities females consistently "underrate", while males consistently "overrate" '.[6]

6.4.1 *Evaluation of services*

The greatest trap into which the unwary information worker may fall is to lose sight of the purpose and priorities of the organization itself. For the solo worker, more than any other information specialist, the professional development plan should relate to an evaluation of how well the service being provided matches the needs of the organization. Thus the role of service evaluation in a one-person or one-professional unit is twofold: giving direction to the development of the service and to the personal development of the individual.

Evaluation should not be feared. Surprise findings may lead you to shift priorities in the management of resources (including time) in ways that could not have been envisaged. Certainly evidence of gaps and deficiencies is likely to emerge; nothing could be more helpful as an indicator of areas for professional development.

Surprisingly little of the material on evaluation of information services is tailored to meet the needs of small specialized services. 'The person who comes up with appropriate effectiveness measures for library services is going to be our patron saint!' writes St Clair.[7] Regrettably Cronin's preliminary work on a 'self-evaluation package' received little support,[8] though there is no need to be daunted by the absence of checklists and formulae. 'Reading around' the subject will help and, in any case, Cronin observed that evaluation is a matter of 'applied commonsense'.[9]

'The purpose of evaluation is to relate performance to objectives.'[10] Effective evaluation is guided by a clear understanding of the purposes which the organization seeks to achieve through the information unit, and recognition of the priority accorded to each. Williamson (1993) emphasizes that written aims and objectives, business plans, policy documents and so on, are essential tools for the library trainer[11] – and as a solo operator you are the library trainer! Ideally, to quote Lawes, 'We should set the goals and criteria right from the beginning and then determine how we are matching our services to them',[12] but it is never too late to start on the process of agreeing explicit goals with your management.

6.4.2 *Methods*

Time is precious – too precious to waste on providing services which do not 'measure up', but also too precious to start collecting statistics *ad infinitum*. Rather than 'using a hammer to crack a nut' the amount of time and effort expended on measuring the performance of different aspects of the service should reflect their level of priority.

A number of mechanisms can be used to build up a picture of the success of the service. The aim should be to collect data which informs decision-making. It is desirable to combine continuous monitoring of certain areas of the service with 'snapshots' of other aspects. For instance, some record of journal articles requested from outside sources will be necessary anyway, and in the long term will allow analysis of those titles most in demand, contributing to an evaluation of subscriptions. SDI services might be evaluated by means of continuous monitoring of 'take-up' or by an occasional review of user satisfaction.

Direct approaches to users are informative, whether carried out informally or formally. User surveys are helpful, provided they are conducted infrequently. Questionnaires may supplement discussions at staff meetings and in 'library committee' (if there is one). Additionally they may be useful as a trigger to introduce changes to the service. User surveys often provide a written record of 'customer satisfaction' from which the information worker can quote.

6.4.3 Projected needs of the employer

Many organizations experience radical changes in direction, therefore priorities shift over time. Obviously the value of the information service depends upon keeping your 'finger on the pulse'; so does your ability to analyse present and future development needs. A number of analytical tools have been developed to assist the management of change. PEST and SWOT, outlined below, are especially relevant. In this respect, time spent reading a few key texts on management may be more profitable than thumbing through a favourite journal on librarianship.

Analysis of the Political/legal, Economic, Socio-cultural and Technological (PEST) influences upon the organization may help to establish the long-term 'drivers' of change and to examine the differential impact of external influences upon the organization.[13] Diverse factors may be significant – including market competition, demographic factors and the political climate.

SWOT analysis is a practical means of looking at the resources of the organization in the light of external influences to reveal Strengths, Weaknesses, Opportunities and Threats.[14] Accordingly strategies can be formulated to match strengths to opportunities, minimizing weaknesses.

Webb remarks upon the importance of a keen awareness of the organization's changing activities, and future needs, to the assessment of training needs.[15] Informal networks are a mine of information, but it is also important to seek out opportunities to discuss the organization's plans for the future. This allows the library manager to project the information services likely to be required, and identify personal development needs accordingly.

6.4.4 Review the job description

Having evaluated the service, and looked to the future of the organization and the unit, the focus can switch to a review of current roles and responsibilities, which may also reveal areas for personal professional development.

However inexpertly written by a 'lay' manager struggling to express and encompass the organization's requirements, the job description remains an important document. It can be a salutary reminder of expectations and priorities, highlighting areas which have begun to monopolize resources to an inappropriate degree, and indicating areas which have received insufficient attention, or in which the service has yet to be developed. Similarly, access to the person specification (if there is one) may offer new insight into the skills, knowledge and attitudes originally expected of the postholder.

6.4.5 Review current work

Element A of Stage 1 of The Library Association's Personal Profile document,[16] given in Appendix 7, is one tool to review current work and areas for professional development. As you review the key areas of your work consider:

- Are you satisfied with your present performance?
- In which areas could you make improvements?
- What additional skills or knowledge are needed to achieve improvements?

The checklist of the development needs of solo information professionals (see section 4.7.1) may help to identify specific areas in which further development is required.

Webb shows the value of noting how much you like or dislike specific tasks.[17] Once you can recognize what it is that you dislike about certain activities, you can plan to develop the service, or yourself, in ways which will remedy the situation. Options might include buying-in a service, changing or delegating a process, developing new skills or confronting personal attitudes.

6.4.6 Techniques to review current performance

Different techniques of analysis suit different people. If you are disappointed by the amount, or quality, of information elicited from the review of current work it may be helpful to try one or two other techniques:

Time log
For a period (perhaps a week or a month) log the demands upon your time, perhaps categorizing the areas as appropriate.

Critical incident technique
Each day, or week, record the most difficult activity or task which you undertook. While you have the page open, make a note too of successes, however minor.

Complaints
Always take heed of complaints, however veiled, and be alert for any pattern which begins to emerge from them.

Each of the above approaches helps to identify 'problem areas': procedures which call for greater efficiency, areas in which performance might be more effective, and any areas in which you and your users are experiencing real difficulties.

6.4.7 A personal SWOT analysis

Successful career planning revolves around matching individual strengths and weaknesses with present, and probable, opportunities and threats. Just as you can carry out a SWOT analysis of the information service (see section 6.4.3 above) so the same approach may be applied to personal development. This calls for an appraisal of personal capabilities (e.g. technical abilities, interpersonal and management skills) plus an assessment of weaknesses and gaps in competence reached in the light of matching strengths to perceived opportunities.

Element B of Stage 1 of The Library Association's Personal Profile,[18] given in Appendix 8, is intended to help you anticipate new roles which you may assume in the future, within your present post or as a result of a career move.

It is important to use a 'wide-angled lens' when looking at strengths and weaknesses, bringing skills and talents not exploited at present into the picture. Moreover, current strengths may reflect previous experience rather than real aptitudes and, in any case, may not be consistent with those personal values and interests on which you wish to base your future.

6.5 Prepare the plan

Armed with the information yielded by taking a systematic look at the present, and towards the future, the next step is to draw up a personal plan. Once it is possible to place an assessment of personal skills into the context of organizational needs, professional trends, personal opportunities and career preferences, it is surprisingly straightforward to identify and prioritize personal development needs.

6.5.1 *Personal goals*

The need to set goals in order to motivate personal professional development has already been considered (see section 5.4).

Some people respond best to choosing a very specific long-term goal, such as gaining a higher degree in managing health information or expanding the role of school librarian in anticipation of a future role as learning resources centre manager. The individual is then able to establish short-term objectives which will, of themselves, contribute to professional development. For instance, the school librarian might plan to become more proficient in using the hardware, and more familiar with the software already in school, and take steps to keep up to date with new resources and equipment coming on to the market.

Others prefer to set more general goals, for example, to broaden their understanding of information technology. Specific targets might be improving proficiency in online searching, becoming familiar with CD-ROM or the Internet!

Accomplishment of these goals may well require the action, commitment and support of other people, especially those 'nearest and dearest'.

6.5.2 *Set goals*

Obviously personal goals cannot be cast in tablets of stone; nevertheless personal professional development will only be achieved by purposeful endeavour directed at specific aims. A straightforward strategy for effective goal-setting is to:[19]

- identify weaknesses and gaps in skills or knowledge;

- decide how to measure performance/validate achievements;
- make a note of the base-line: current performance/level of skill or knowledge;
- set a long-term goal, or goals;
- identify short-term objectives;
- identify the actions needed to reach each objective;
- make a realistic assessment of obstacles you will encounter;
- inform an authority figure, whom you respect, of your aims.

6.5.3 *Monitor progress*

Most people find it helpful to enlist the support of others on whom they can rely for encouragement, and with whom they can share the pleasure of their progress and success.

Reviewing the development plan, monitoring progress, comparing performance and achievements with the base-line, are all part of the process. 'Evaluation should be an on-going and integral part', to quote guidelines for quality in continuing education adopted by the American Library Association in 1988.[20] SCOLE (the Standing Committee on Library Education) enumerated those points to which individuals must give special attention in planning and evaluating continuing education activities. See Appendix 9.

6.6 Putting the plan into practice

There is more than one way to crack a walnut and there are several different ways of categorizing professional development needs – and many different ways of meeting them. The solo librarian or information officer has to be more inventive than most in seeking out opportunities for personal development, and has reason to be more critical than most in terms of selecting formal opportunities for professional development.

References

1 The Library Association, *Your personal profile. The framework for continuing professional development*, The Library Association, 1992.
2 Timm, P. R., *Successful self-management: a sound approach to personal effectiveness*, Kogan Page, 1987.
3 Davie, G., *Religion in Britain since 1945: believing without belonging*, Blackwell, 1994.
4 Redman, W., *Portfolios for development: a guide for trainers and managers*, Kogan Page, 1994.
5 Pedler, M., Burgoyne, J. and Boydell, T. (eds.), *Applying self-development in organizations*, Prentice Hall, 1988.
6 Ibid.
7 St Clair, G., 'The times they are a-changin' . . . ', *Library manager*, Dec. 1994, issue 2.
8 Cronin, B., 'Performance measurement and information management', *Aslib proceedings*, **34** (5), 1982, 227–36.
9 Ibid.
10 Ibid.
11 Williamson, M., *Training needs analysis*, Library Association Publishing, 1993.
12 St Clair, op. cit.

13 Johnson, G. and Scholes, K., *Exploring corporate strategy*, 3rd edn, Prentice Hall International, 1993.

14 Ibid.

15 Casteleyn, M. and Webb, S. P., *Promoting excellence: personnel management and staff development in libraries*, Bowker-Saur, 1993.

16 The Library Association, op. cit.

17 Webb, S. P., *Personal development in information work*, 2nd edn, Aslib, 1991.

18 The Library Association, op. cit.

19 Robertson, I. T., Smith, M. and Cooper, D., *Motivation: strategies, theory and practice*, 2nd edn, Institute of Personnel Management, 1992.

20 Continuing Education Subcommittee of the Standing Committee on Library Education (SCOLE), *Guidelines for quality in continuing education for information, library and media personnel*, American Library Association, 1988.

Opportunities for personal professional development

Most opportunities for personal professional development are relatively inexpensive, but all require the commitment of time: work time and personal time, time to prepare beforehand and time to reflect afterwards.

Having established personal development needs, individuals will need to identify appropriate methods of achieving each aspect of the development plan. A balanced mix of formal and informal learning methods, drawing on a range of activities and approaches, is desirable. Compromises may have to be made, matching personal need to organizational and personal resources. However, with an understanding of personal learning style, and a good relationship with the person responsible for the training budget, a favourable climate for professional development can be achieved.

7.1 Preferred learning style

To make the best possible use of opportunities for professional development, the individual is well advised to invest just a little time in thinking about the act of learning.

Mumford insists 'that *learning how to learn* is itself a major managerial requirement'.[1] Recognition of preferred styles of learning has many significant benefits: increasing confidence, motivation and capacity to learn and, not least, equipping the individual 'to make conscious choices about activities in terms of whether they believe themselves likely to learn from them'.[2]

Two models of learning styles are 'in vogue', each supported by a simple diagnostic tool. Originally Kolb developed the experiential learning cycle (see section 7.9). The Learning Style Inventory[3] was devised to measure an individual's relative reliance on each of four styles. Later Honey and Mumford developed a Learning Styles Questionnaire[4] which helps learners to see themselves as an activist, a reflector, a theorist or a pragmatist.

The activist will need opportunities to get involved in a task while the reflector will be most interested in the communal review of what has taken place. The theorist needs to be able to see the subject in the context of a system or theory, and for the pragmatist, learning will be triggered by perceiving the links between the course and tasks ahead at the workplace.

Recognition of personal learning preferences can be liberating – illuminating memories of situations in which you have had difficulty 'taking something on board', and enabling you 'to extend, to take advantage of, a wider variety of opportunities to learn'.[5]

Those working in large organizations will be able to access one of these means of assessing personal learning styles via the training section or personnel department. For further reading see the section on learning in the Select Bibliography.

7.2   Relationships with managers and training departments

Training, i.e. identifying and remedying gaps in competencies and skills required to function in a post, has traditionally been seen as the role of line management. The manager will have (or at least be able to locate) the key to some resources for training, and will also be able to facilitate wider opportunities for professional development.

The difficulty with which many managers of solo workers comprehend the role asked of the information unit has already been noted in section 6.4.4. Challenging as it may be, the task is for the solo information professional to explain ways in which performance might be strengthened by some means of continuing education, in order to equip the individual to make improvements and introduce new services to meet the information needs of the organization.

Solo librarians and information scientists need to build up a rapport with training managers, remembering that they have much to gain from interdisciplinary training events as from opportunities tailored for information specialists (see section 7.4.2).

Managers, trainers and anyone else 'holding the purse-strings' will be keen to distinguish between genuine 'needs' and 'wishes' for personal development, and to differentiate between 'training needs' and 'education needs'.[6] The value of pursuing further qualifications is discussed in Chapter 8.

7.2.1   *The training 'culture'*

Obviously each organization has its own training 'culture' which the individual can 'play' to advantage. Participating in professional meetings and taking on committee responsibilities may be seen as good 'PR' within one organization; elsewhere concern may be expressed at 'outside' professional interests encroaching upon the workload. Some organizations will finance external professional courses but discourage informal visits to specialized library services, and vice-versa.

7.2.2   *Induction training*

The importance of getting professional development on to the agenda at an early stage has already been suggested (see section 3.2.4). Librarians and information workers who are not greeted by at least the skeleton of an induction programme need to act swiftly, and be ready to draw up and negotiate their own programme. It will be helpful to include some shadowing (see section 7.4.3) as well as external visits (see section 7.6.2).

7.3   The experience of one-person/one-professional librarians

The late 1980s saw the completion of several surveys into training preferences and practice which helped to illuminate the experience of solo librarians (in addition to Williamson's 1987 study, discussed in section 4.6 and the work by Collins and Shuter discussed in section 5.1).

7.3.1   *Special libraries*

Of respondents to Slater's 1986 survey[7] of training practice in special libraries, 39% managed one-person or one-professional units. For 90% of these the training situation was unsatisfactory; 71% received no in-house training at all.

Slater found 'OMBs' to be doubly deprived, for they also reported the lowest level of attendance at external short courses of all the librarians surveyed. Nevertheless 79% of solo professionals did participate in short courses; 14% attended such events 'frequently', 48% 'sometimes'.[8]

The survey offers evidence of the preferences of solo information specialists which may still be 'news' to some providers of continuing education. For instance, solo workers are particularly subject to seasonal pressures and find it easiest to attend courses held between February and April or in October and November. Not surprisingly, the smaller the unit, the shorter the length of course required – reflecting practical difficulties in arranging 'cover'.[9]

7.3.2 *School libraries*

MacDougall, Lewins and Tseng's complementary research[10] showed that school librarians were somewhat under-represented at external events, in comparison with colleagues in professional, academic and public libraries. Attendance at short courses and conferences accounted for only 19% of their continuing education activities, although participation in seminars and meetings accounted for another 24%. By contrast more than half of the activities reported took the form of in-service training.

7.4 **Work-based opportunities**

In 1988 Ritchie reported on a survey of members of The Library Association, employed in libraries of all sizes, regarding attitudes to management development.[11] Ritchie found that librarians value practical, work-based activities as the most useful for career development. Actual work experience was regarded as the most important method by far. Liaison with colleagues and in-service training scored highly, followed by visits to other information units. Job rotation and short courses in librarianship were ranked joint fifth place, followed by reading professional literature.

7.4.1 *Work within the one-person/one-professional unit*

Unlikely as it may appear at first glance, the greatest opportunity for personal professional development lies within the job itself. Solo information workers enjoy the rare privilege of being able to manage every aspect of an information service while remaining in direct contact with its users. There is tremendous scope for initiating and planning services, for improving procedures, and for dispensing with activities which are ineffective.

Confidence will grow in response to personal achievements in managing the unit. Inevitably, some aspects of personal development will be achieved by 'incidental learning', through painful experiences from which hard lessons are learned – as well as successful initiatives blessed by 'a stroke of luck' which can be 'programmed in' to the next venture. Retrospection is an important way of learning from experiences at work – taking the time to consider and reach conclusions about events at work. This is one of the strengths of mentoring (see section 7.4.5).

Webb[12] has written a comprehensive account of the ways in which librarians and information workers can make use of opportunities which arise as an integral part of their work in creating, providing and enhancing services to satisfy the information needs of the organization. As an example, Webb uses the interview as an analogy for the many other work situations in which interpersonal skills may be developed.

7.4.2   *In-house training*

In small organizations responsibility for oversight of a training budget is often assigned to an individual (see section 7.2). Large employers will have a training section with staff who can 'buy-in', and sometimes provide, in-house courses.

In the light of Slater's report on the training situation for staff of one-person units (see section 7.3.1), it is essential for solo workers in special libraries to persuade their managers of the benefits of participation in internal training programmes. In-house training (whether on health and safety, report writing, word-processing or more sophisticated approaches to communication, information technology and management) creates opportunities for the solo worker to develop personal networks within the organization, to deepen understanding of the information needs of users, and to promote the information service. Learning alongside staff from other professional backgrounds builds networks and encourages creative thinking.

7.4.3   *Shadowing*

The mention of any professional group will conjure up a stereotypical image. Accountants, barristers, civil engineers, health visitors, research chemists, social workers and teachers may have less reason to relish their public image than librarians! All information workers will recognize the need to overcome the misunderstandings which such images foster, but for one-person operators this is an imperative.

The value of spending several hours shadowing a representative of each of the key disciplines served by the information unit cannot be overestimated. Shadowing provides an opportunity to learn about the work of users of the service, dispel myths, confront personal assumptions and sharpen up understanding of the information needs of clients. It helps the information worker to move beyond the picture presented by current demands upon the information unit, recognizing needs that have not yet been perceived, to identify ways in which services can be improved.

It is easiest to make this kind of request soon after taking up a post, since shadowing also provides an opportunity to survey attitudes and expectations of the unit, as well as patterns of use. Nevertheless, it can be a sensible approach at times when new developments in the service are being considered.

7.4.4   *Staff exchanges*

While few solo information workers are in a position to arrange an exchange, some one-person librarians, who may never have considered such an initiative, could take advantage of this means of personal professional development. Exchanges are most practical within large companies which boast more than one information unit and within medical libraries, where it may be possible to exchange roles with a colleague in the same region.

In both cases the employer will retain the services of an information worker who has specialized in the field, and benefit from a fresh look at systems and services. Companies can also look towards ensuring common standards of provision across the organization. For the individual, effecting an exchange will call for imagination, persuasion and persistence, but it can be most instructive to 'swop desks' with a colleague.

7.4.5 *Mentors*

'Mentoring is a way of helping another understand more fully, and learn more comprehensively from, their day to day experience', explains Hamilton.[13]

Although mentoring is such a valuable developmental tool, it features more as a matter of discussion than practice among information professionals. A recent survey by the Industrial Society[14] reported that formal mentoring schemes were established in 40% of the organizations involved. Accordingly, information workers may be able to 'ride on the coat-tails' of this advance by investigating whether formal arrangements are already in place within the employing organization.

Fisher observes that informal mentoring is 'the more common practice'.[15] Individuals may be able to reach an informal arrangement with a trusted and respected information specialist employed outside the organization.

7.4.6 *Writing and research*

'The experience of organizing one's thoughts and submitting them to public scrutiny, no matter how small the audience, is a significant dimension of staff development opportunities', observed Weber.[16]

In-house newsletters are an obvious channel of communication with users. Offers to supply a regular 'news' item from the information unit will almost certainly be welcomed, and pave the way for detailed reviews of the service.

The professional press offers other opportunities. Managers of one-person units can learn from the ingenuity of each other, adopting and adapting approaches. Thus there is real value in sharing personal experience of introducing new software, establishing a new service, designing a new unit and so on. In addition, a number of solo information workers are employed in specialized areas which evoke curiosity among other professionals, perhaps because of a love of cricket or an interest in cathedrals and historic houses. A wider audience will be fascinated to read an article on the collections held, their use and users, and specific problems.

Most journals issue notes on style for authors. Writers need to study the format and approach of articles in the journal in which they hope to be published. Whatever the motivation to write, there is no doubt that a blank page or screen concentrates the mind wonderfully, prompting the individual to analyse and resolve weaknesses within the service being described.

7.4.7 *Committee work*

An understanding of how to work effectively in groups is critical to career progression. All professions spend a considerable amount of time in one sort of group or another, and many decisions are made within meetings. One-person operators may be expected to participate in various committees, project teams and working parties within the organization and to represent the interests of the employer on external committees.

Inevitably, solo information professionals have less opportunity to practise group work within the relative safety of peer groups than the staff of large information services. Thus it will be helpful to look at other means of developing the necessary skills. Joining the committee of one of the many professional groups which need ideas and energy can help the individual to develop subject expertise, maintain motivation and gain confidence. Equally, informal learning through chairing the playgroup committee, serving as entertainments officer for the sports club, or acting as secretary to the district church council, will help. Some people find it more fruitful, and less painful, to seek out formal opportunities to study group processes and team-building (which has attracted more interest in recent years) rather than relying purely on experience and observation.

7.5 Involvement in professional activities

The professional isolation inherent in the work of the solo information manager should encourage involvement in professional activities.

St Clair and Williamson (1992) emphasize the sense of affirmation which membership of a professional association confers.[17] Moreover there is a strong case for becoming involved in the activities of one, or more, of the professional bodies (see section 7.4.7). As well as providing a wealth of services, and access to resources, Webb has shown that taking an active interest in wider professional matters is stimulating and beneficial, offering enormous scope for professional development.[18] See sections 3.4.1 and 3.5.

7.6 Informal learning

Whatever the limitations on formal work-based and work-funded development programmes, everyone can benefit from informal opportunities for professional development. In small units skilful exploitation of self-directed methods of learning (notably through developing networks, visits and professional reading) is vital.

7.6.1 Personal networks

One approach open to every librarian and information specialist who works alone is to develop and nurture the 'invisible college'. The crucial importance of building interpersonal networks has been explored in Chapter 3. Investing time and goodwill in these networks pays dividends, allowing the solo librarian to discuss professional concerns, gain advice from fellow information workers, and keep up to date with new developments.

7.6.2 Visits

Visits are an invaluable means of professional development. The importance of visiting other information services to build informal networks has been discussed (see section 3.2.3). Obviously managers of one-person and one-professional units will benefit from visiting large academic and public library services within the area, as well as specialized information services operating in the same field.

Both informal visits, arranged personally, or formal visits as part of a group, can offer an opportunity to select stock, assess online services and CD-ROMs, review systems for disseminating information, consider alternative forms of library 'housekeeping' (such as periodicals management, acquisitions and circulation systems) and to recognize that all information units have their problems!

7.6.3 *Reading*

Reading is by far the most accessible means of personal professional development. The Bombay study[19] found that reading was the most common strategy to acquire additional knowledge and skills, used by 59% of respondents. Nevertheless it has to be admitted that 'what we regularly do for those we serve is exactly what we fail to do for ourselves'. Matarazzo notes the irony of the failure of many information professionals to 'regularly scan periodicals and the like' in order to stay abreast of the latest information in the field.[20]

For solo librarians and information specialists this is not just a question of allocating regular slots of time in which to read (probably over coffee, on the train and in bed, as well as in worktime) but also of gaining access to material in the first place. Isolated information professionals have a particular need to scan current literature columns and book reviews, request searches, and develop their own skills as purposive library users. In order to support personal development, and function effectively as an informed manager, solo professionals should have no qualms about exploiting all the information services to which they have access (including BLISS and the public library).

Asking the employer to fund an appropriate subscription is a good starting point. It may also be possible to use informal networks and visits to secure a place on the end of the circulation list of professional journals taken by a neighbouring library; willingness to circulate those periodicals to which the individual subscribes will help. There is plenty of potential for this type of cooperation between small units, for example exchanging Institute of Information Science mailings in return for those from The Library Association. The benefits of the publications which derive from professional membership have already been noted (see section 3.4).

The Select bibliography suggests further reading on key areas for professional development for solo workers.

7.7 Short courses and exhibitions

'One-man band personnel have above average difficulty in actually attending courses', to quote Slater.[21] Given the wealth of other opportunities for professional development, and the poor quality of some courses, this is not the end of the world. Nor is it an excuse: no-one is indispensable, not even the solo information worker. Precisely the same arrangements that are made to cover during annual leave and sickness can prevail for the duration of a short course. If it is not seen as essential to cover absence at these times then one more day cannot make things worse – but might help the beleaguered professional to change matters for the better.

Nevertheless it can be hard to match the benefits of a well-planned, well-led course. Thus it is important to seek funding to attend external events which meet the needs and priorities already identified in the personal development plan.

It can be difficult to select suitable courses, as solo information managers may be asked to take an imaginative leap to apply the material offered to their own situation . . . Reporting on one session at a study day for medical librarians, Prior noted that although the speaker 'particularly emphasized the economics of scale, some of the audience had difficulty in scaling up the concepts from a staff of two to the 22 she manages'.[22]

It is more than reasonable to request further information from the organizer before embarking on the process of convincing 'the piper' to meet the cost of fees, travelling expenses, absence and staff. Sufficient information is needed to enable the applicant to gauge the expertise of the course provider(s), ensure that the programme is relevant and at an appropriate level, and that its structure will suit the way in which the individual learns best (see section 7.1).

Access to information about short courses is not quite as straightforward as it may appear – an observation confirmed by Williamson's (1991) finding that '28% of OMBs thought there was not enough information available on continuing education courses'.[23] Scanning as wide a range of professional journals as possible helps to overcome this problem, but it is also useful to contact relevant training agencies, requesting inclusion on the mailing list. Some examples are given in Appendix 3.

To gain the most value from a course, Ray (1991) recommends thoughtful preparation.[24] Before attending, keep a diary on the subject in hand, noting current activities and concerns, even how long it takes. Baddock is a keen advocate of relaxed discussion over a beer, remembering that 'at least 40% of what you gain will come from your colleagues in an informal manner during group discussions and in the bar afterwards'.[25]

7.7.1 *The professional bodies*

Aslib, the Institute of Information Scientists and The Library Association each run continuing education events. 'Off the record', solo workers tend to subscribe to the view that these events are expensive. Speaking of one of these three, an OMB in Slater's survey commented, 'How they get away with charging such amazing high prices and still get customers baffles me . . . [They] should provide free courses to members'.[26] Nevertheless, the professional bodies provide varied programmes which hold some interest for solo practitioners (some 16% of participants in Library Association courses work in special libraries).

The School Library Association offers one-day training courses at very reasonable prices, comparable to the cost of attending events organized by the special interest groups of the other professional bodies. Group events will also be particularly attractive to solo professionals because of their specialist focus.

Joan Williamson runs training sessions for one-person librarians, usually on behalf of one of the special groups, concentrating on management issues and personal effectiveness. Appendix 10 gives a sample of material used in sessions on time management.

7.7.2 *Training agencies*

One company, TFPL Ltd, has a track record of providing events geared to the needs of one-person operators, reflecting the interest of solo professionals in aspects of personal development and in sector-based training, for example in business information.

A number of training consultancies now run continuing education events, from courses to exhibitions, which are frequently publicized in the *Library Association record*.

Although many organizations outside information work offer relevant short courses, the fact is that most solo information workers will be limited by a tight budget, which puts these out of reach. Some well-established bodies, like the Tavistock Institute, offer realistically priced programmes (such as their Group Relations Study Group) in addition to more prestigious events. See Appendix 3.

7.7.3 Local providers

Providers of training courses at the local level come in all shapes and sizes and offer a surprising range of opportunities, many at low cost. The five examples in the ABC from central Buckinghamshire, which follows, give an indication of the wealth of local opportunities. Each of these organizations holds short courses throughout the year:

- *Adult education*: the value of evening classes and Saturday workshops should not be dismissed. Appendix 10 gives sample material from one trainer, Sue Germain, who leads courses and workshops on Assertiveness.
- *Aylesbury College*: the business administration and computing programme of short courses includes desktop publishing, setting up a local area network, word processing and MS-DOS and Windows for beginners.
- *BBi*: offers a varied programme of low-cost training events (see section 3.3.1).
- *Chamber of Commerce*: Thames Valley CCi Training Ltd offers a comprehensive programme including courses on communication, e.g. assertiveness and writing, and management, e.g. time management and presentation skills.
- *Chiltern Christian Training Programme*: CCTP organizes training and learning opportunities to help people reach their full potential. The Open University short course on managing stress and a basic workshop on Myers-Briggs may run alongside courses on spiritual topics.

One further point is that isolated professionals with the initiative to ask may find that they are welcome to participate in training events run by the public library service, the nearby university or within the National Health Service region. In addition the training officer, or staff of the personnel department, may be able to recommend courses on specific topics.

Courses held within the area offer the additional advantage of extending the 'invisible college'. Thus solo information providers will be keen to look out for training providers on their own 'doorstep'. The organizations named here, as examples, are listed in Appendix 3.

7.7.4 Exhibitions

Library and information professionals have a particular interest in exhibitions. Just as the exhibition will be one of the attractions at large conferences, so the provision of learning opportunities (demonstrations, lectures, workshops) is increasingly part of the attraction of exhibitions.

There are several big events each year and the cost is usually minimal. Attendance allows the information worker to see the latest in equipment, technology or publications, to chat with sales personnel, and to pre-arrange meetings with distant colleagues.

Advance preparation is advisable: a note of questions about a particular system and a list of stock gaps will ensure that the occasion is used to full advantage.

7.8 Further study

Opportunities to obtain further qualifications are considered separately in Chapter 8. However there are other means of study, such as computer assisted learning and, most notably, distance education. Both have keen advocates but neither method has been greeted enthusiastically by the profession at large.

7.8.1 *Computer assisted learning*

The Special Libraries Association has successfully launched some interactive courses in their self-study programme, including material on writing[27] and time management.[28] These provide feedback which cannot be achieved by the workbook format which is also available. It remains to be seen whether solo information specialists in Britain will choose to pursue professional development at their unit's Apple Macintosh or IBM-compatible computer.

7.8.2 *Distance education*

The principal drawback of distance education for the lone information professional is the risk that it too will be carried out in isolation. Admittedly the Open University appoints tutors, and holds its summer schools to overcome this. Similarly, an annual residential study school is an integral part of the Masters courses at Aberystwyth. These are reported to be 'an extremely popular and effective way for library workers to . . . advance their career prospects'.[29] (See section 8.3.1)

While distance education is growing in popularity in some countries, especially in Australia, the choice for potential students in the United Kingdom remains limited, with little change from those identified by Haythornthwaite and White in 1989.[30] The Society of Indexers continues to offer an open learning course which may be of interest to some information workers. One addition is the package on financial management from NTG/SCET.[31] It is assumed that individuals using this package, which is designed for staff of large public services but applicable elsewhere, will be supported by their line manager or a mentor.

7.9 The learning cycle

Whichever means of personal development are used, Kolb's learning cycle is a useful model by which to interpret how learning is achieved. Four definite stages can be observed in the learning process. Following on from the actual experience (for example a project, visit, reading or course) a period of observation, reflection, and perhaps the collection of data, is needed. Further exploration of the principles involved, and analysis of data collected, allows assimilation of what has been learned. This can lead on to action – when new ideas and knowledge can be tested in practice, and new learning needs defined. See Appendix 11.

However busy, librarians and information specialists have to face up to the fact that professional development is not achieved by a series of 'one-off' events. Time is needed to work through these stages. Otherwise the initial effort invested in the actual activity may be unproductive, and opportunities squandered.

References

1 Mumford, A., 'Enhancing your learning skills – a note of guidance for managers', in Wood, S. (ed.), *Continuous development: the path to improved performance*, Institute of Personnel Management, 1988.
2 Ibid.
3 Pont, A. M., *Developing effective training skills*, McGraw-Hill, 1991.
4 Ibid.
5 Mumford, op. cit.
6 Williamson, M., *Training needs analysis*, Library Association Publishing, 1993.
7 Slater, M., *Internal training and external short courses: a study of informal continuing education in the special library/information field*, British Library, 1988. British Library Research Paper 52.
8 Ibid.
9 Ibid.
10 MacDougall, J., Lewins, H. and Tseng, G., *Continuing education and training opportunities in librarianship: a study of participation, benefits and defects*, British Library Research and Development Department, 1990. British Library Research Paper 74.
11 Ritchie, S., *Training and management development in librarianship*, British Library, 1988. Library and Information Research Report 34.
12 Webb, S. P., *Personal development in information work*, 2nd edn, Aslib, 1991.
13 Hamilton, R., *Mentoring: a practical guide to the skills of mentoring*, The Industrial Society, 1993.
14 Fisher, B., *Mentoring*, Library Association Publishing, 1994.
15 Ibid.
16 Weber, D. C., 'The dynamics of the library environment for professional staff growth', reprinted in Layzell Ward, P. (ed.), *The professional development of the librarian and information worker*, Aslib, 1980.
17 St Clair, G. and Williamson, J., *Managing the new one-person library*, 2nd edn, Bowker-Saur, 1992.
18 Webb, op. cit.
19 Jani, N., Parekh, H. and Sen, B., 'Individual perceptions of professional advancement', *Libri*, **41** (3), 1991, 183–93.
20 Matarazzo, J. M., 'Continuing professional education', *Special libraries*, **78** (4), Fall 1987, 247–50.
21 Slater, op. cit.
22 Prior, P., 'Meetings reports: postgraduate medical education and libraries, 24 November 1993, Bristol', *Health libraries review*, **11** (1), March 1994, 64–6.
23 Williamson, J., 'One person libraries and information units: their education and training needs', *Library & information research news*, **14** (5), Summer 1991, 12–19.
24 Ray, L., *How to measure training effectiveness*, 2nd edn, Gower, 1991.
25 Baddock, C., *P.D.R. blues: beating the professional development report bugbear*, Colin Baddock Training Consultancy, 1989.
26 Slater, op. cit.

27 Wessell, D., *Grace under pressure: writing with clarity, conciseness and impact*, Special Libraries Association, 1989.
28 Berner, A., *Time management in the small library: a self-study program*, Special Libraries Association, 1988.
29 Thomas, C., 'Info on distance learning', letter published in the *Library Association record*, **97** (2), February 1995, 86.
30 Haythornthwaite, J. A. and White, F. C. P., *Distance education in library and information studies*, British Library Research and Development Department, 1989. British Library Research Paper 50.
31 Foggett, T. and Bartlett, G., *Financial management for librarians*, NTG/SCET, 1993.

 **Pursuing qualifications**

'Danger: Obsolescence in the Marketplace', warned Weingand more than a decade ago, noting that the 'average "shelf-life" of a degree today is approximately five years'.[1]

Solo information workers may well be more vulnerable to the vicissitudes of that marketplace than other library and information professionals. Accordingly, it is important to review the marketability of your own package of skills and qualifications from time to time.

8.1 **Formal qualifications in library and information work**

Significant numbers of solo librarians have not pursued formal qualifications in librarianship or information science, offering instead specialized experience and expertise, often accompanied by relevant academic qualifications.

Traditionally, special libraries have recruited staff with specialist qualifications and have not necessarily required qualifications in librarianship or information science.[2] This is reflected in Moore's finding that 'skills and experience appear to be more significant in the eyes of employers than formal qualifications.'[3]

Nevertheless the pattern has changed considerably over the past 20 years.[4] The 1981 Department of Education and Science Census[5] recorded that 53% of industrial and commercial librarians did not hold formal qualifications in librarianship. By contrast, in Williamson's sample of one-person units, conducted in 1987,[6] just 25% of the staff had not attended 'library school'.

A reluctance to follow one of the vocational courses is understandable but questionable. Admittedly Moore's study showed that, even where jobs are particularly appropriate for information workers, 'over 70% of employers do not regard library or information qualifications as being essential'. Instead, Moore found that employers rate 'very highly' transferable skills, such as interpersonal communication skills.[7] (See section 3.2.) However some employers are unaware of the full range of qualifications available in the field. Worse still, their difficulty in drawing up a person specification, and probably in expressing the information needs of the organization, is unlikely to make them any more patient with the efforts of a solo librarian ill-equipped for the role.

Those who do not feel motivated to take a course in librarianship or information work may seek comfort in the finding that 'the satisfied OMB' was just as likely *not* to have a qualification in information work, as to have one.[8] Equally they may argue that, in Williamson's survey,[9] few of those without such qualifications expressed a need for further training in information management. However this calls for some thought. Firstly, Williamson observed that many of these respondents 'had no real idea of how to manage an information unit'.[10] Secondly, it seems likely that the weight of demand for further training on information sources and information retrieval, evinced by the study, may be as much a call for basic skills, as for specialized training. Obviously this need is best remedied by following a course in librarianship or information science. See Appendix 3 for sources of further information.

In addition to those accredited courses designed to prepare students for professional practice, there are also a number of courses aimed at the para-professional (see Appendix 3). The introduction of Scottish/National Vocational Qualifications will enable individuals to demonstrate their competence, rather than concentrate on acquiring theoretical knowledge, building the basis of a personal portfolio which may, in time, form the route to a professional qualification in information work.

8.2 Professional qualifications

The pursuit of professional qualifications affirms our own professionalism, confirms it to others, and offers a safeguard for employers who are not familiar with appointing librarians or information scientists.

The processes involved in gaining admission as a full Member of the Institute of Information Scientists, and in meeting the requirements for registration as a Chartered Librarian can make a real contribution to professional development. Despite changes in Library Association regulations since its publication, Baddock's *P.D.R. blues* remains a useful introduction to continuing professional development.[11]

Both bodies offer Fellowship as a higher professional qualification, the award of which indicates a high level of professionalism.

8.2.1 *External supervision: one route to Associateship*

Many inexperienced professionals taking up their first post in a small unit opt to take two years to qualify as a Chartered Librarian (by Route B). There is much to recommend taking the extra time and trouble to locate an external supervisor willing to provide an LA-approved training programme over one year. See 'The Associateship handbook'.[12]

Woolley found that his supervisor not only helped him to tackle the responsibilities of his post, and to identify training needs, but also played an important role in informing his employer of the necessity of continuing professional development.[13]

8.2.2 *Fellowship of The Library Association*

The regulations for admission to the Register as an Associate of The Library Association allow for the submission of a portfolio of evidence of professional development. Wood points out that this option 'has the advantage that it provides a vehicle for progression from Associateship to Fellowship'.[14]

8.3 Further qualifications

Despite Weingand's 'Hazard Warning' library and information staff often appear reluctant to undertake any extended form of study. An investigation of the continuing education activities of academic, public and school library and information staff found that courses of study leading to further qualifications accounted for only 2% of the total.[15] This reticence may be attributed, in part, to some scepticism as to the real value of making the kind of financial, intellectual and time commitment required to gain a further qualification.

8.3.1 Higher degrees in librarianship and information work

A range of higher degrees is now on offer, some reflecting common specialisms of solo librarians. Those within striking distance of library schools offering part-time Masters courses are fortunate. Meanwhile the distance learning courses offered by the University of Wales, Aberystwyth (for example the MSc(Econ) and Diploma: Health Information Management and the MLib: School and Young People's Librarianship) will be of interest to certain solo information workers. See Appendix 3.

8.3.2 Sector-related qualifications

Clearly, it can be necessary for solo workers to enhance their 'academic' credibility in the sector in which they are employed. Thus individuals may be found working towards any one of a host of qualifications, for example in educational technology or health education to name just two fields, while in higher education, solo librarians are to be found working on their own doctorate.

Solo information workers in the commercial sector may be particularly keen to develop their knowledge of languages. On the other hand, given that so many librarians enter scientific and technological libraries on the foundation of a humanities degree, the demand among one-person library managers for greater subject knowledge is not to be wondered at. Open University courses provide one means of developing greater subject knowledge. See Appendix 3.

8.3.3 Management qualifications

Drawing upon the experience of women in British librarianship, Burrington comments that women 'may prefer to opt for a more generally useful qualification such as an MBA, especially if they see this increases their chance of being seen as suitably qualified for management posts in libraries or feel it will give them access to related jobs if work in libraries proves difficult to get'.[16]

8.3.4 The time commitment

'Studying after a long and tiring day is far from ideal and I do not recommend it' is the candid comment from Williamson.[17] Certainly full-time information workers who take on part-time study will rapidly hone their skills in time management.

8.3.5 The financial commitment

Webb's study of UK professional firms[18] found that many paid examination fees, although some restricted this practice to specific qualifications.

'Qualifications of any kind count for more if you were sponsored by your employer', counsels Burrington.[19] This point is not to be disregarded, since course fees represent a major financial commitment.

| 8.3.6 | *Potential financial rewards* |

The principal rewards of further study lie in personal development. Nevertheless the findings of a survey of members of the Institute of Information Scientists offer food for thought.[20] Reporting on the 1994 survey of 954 members, Cropley found that the 'greatest benefits come with higher degrees or professional qualifications which are not information based, perhaps because those represent qualifications specific to the sector worked in, and therefore of recognised value'.

| 8.4 | **Personal rewards** |

The pursuit of a further qualification is more rigorous and demanding than other forms of continuing professional development. By corollary it is also much more rewarding.

Burrington has encouraged female librarians to recount the experience and benefits they have gained from further study, and their anecdotal evidence is of interest to anyone contemplating making this commitment.[21]

Working towards a higher degree calls for sacrifices, of which resigning from choir, quitting squash and foregoing bedtime stories with the offspring may be the least. In return, extended study can open windows in the mind, and doors to new opportunities.

References

1 Weingand, D. E., 'Continuing education', *Journal of education for librarianship*, **24** (4), 1984, 278–82.

2 Moore, N., *The emerging markets for librarians and information workers*, British Library, 1987. Library and Information Research Report 56.

3 East, H., 'Changes in the staffing of UK Special Libraries and information services in the decade 1972–81: a review of the DES Census data', *Journal of documentation*, **39** (4), December 1993, 247–65.

4 See East, op. cit. and Roberts, N., 'Special librarians: job characteristics and work attitudes', *Journal of librarianship*, **11** (1), January 1979, 4–14.

5 East, op. cit.

6 Williamson, J., 'One person libraries and information units: their education and training needs', *Library management*, **9** (5), 1988.

7 Moore, op. cit.

8 Shuter, J., 'The isolated professional', *Information & library manager*, **3** (4), 1984, 106–13.

9 Williamson, J., 'One person libraries and information units: their education and training needs', *Library and information research news*, **14** (5), Summer 1991, 12–19.

10 Ibid.

11 Baddock, C., *P.D.R. blues: beating the professional development report bugbear*, Colin Baddock Training Consultancy, 1989.

12 The Library Association, *Associateship: regulations and notes of Guidance*, The Library Association, 1995.

13 Woolley, M., 'The one-person library: professional development and professional management', *Library management*, **9** (1), 1988.

14 Wood, K., 'More flexible routes to LA qualifications', *Library Association record*, **97** (1), January 1995, 30–3.

15 MacDougall, J., Lewins, H. and Tseng, G., *Continuing education and*

training opportunities in librarianship: a study of participation, benefits and defects, British Library Research & Development Department, 1990. British Library Research Paper 74.

16 Burrington, G., *Equally good: women in British librarianship*, AAL, 1993.

17 Ibid.

18 Webb, S. P., *Best practice?: continuing professional development for library/information staff in UK professional firms*, British Library 1991. British Library Research & Development Report 6039.

19 Burrington, op. cit.

20 Cropley, J., 'Institute of Information Scientists Remuneration Survey 1994', *Inform*, 165, June 1994, Supplement.

21 Burrington, op. cit.

 # The future: career development

Asked about career plans, most people look slightly uncomfortable. They have not given the matter too much thought; probably past career moves were made in a haphazard unplanned manner. Even shrewd opportunism is negated, described as a 'stroke of luck'. Clearly there is room to be more focused, and less self-effacing, in approaching career development.

Job satisfaction is an entirely personal measurement of an individual's assessment of 'The Job'. There will be solo information specialists who have found the ideal niche for their talents, and have no wish to seek another before retirement, whatever limitations this may impose upon them. Their interest in personal professional development is not diminished by this confident choice; rather it may enable them to predict their development needs and plan a satisfying programme with greater certainty.

Librarians and information workers who aspire to 'moving on and up' need to look ahead with realistic expectations, otherwise they run the risk of becoming dissatisfied and demotivated. A finely balanced combination of vision and realism is required, recognizing the opportunities and constraints for career advancement within the employing organization, and appreciating and exploiting all opportunities for personal professional development within the current post.

A single-person information unit within a dynamic, expanding company is more likely to hold opportunities for internal promotion than a mature company which is not planning on growth. Similarly, employment in the pharmaceutical industry or within the media seems more likely to offer opportunities to move 'on and up' into a larger service elsewhere, than work in schools. However, there might be an opportunity for a school librarian to assume additional responsibility for all technical and learning resources, including managing technical staff.

To quote Brown, 'the need for awareness of opportunities before they arise, the ability to create them and the confidence to seize them, are valuable attributes to successful career planning'.[1]

9.1 Influencing promotion and career advancement

It is vital not to fall into the trap of believing that promotion is a just reward for good performance!

Harvey Coleman's research[2] showed that three factors, of widely different levels of significance, contribute to an individual's chances of promotion:

- 10% professional performance
- 30% professional image: keen? interested? coping? confused?
- 60% professional exposure: contacts, 'visibility', professional profile

9.2 The career pattern of solo librarians

An American survey by OPL Resources Ltd[3] showed that around half of one-person librarians are in the relatively early stages of their career, having been involved in information work for less than ten years.

On average, library and information workers stay in a specific post for between five and six years (5.55 years for women and 6.2 years for men).[4] Although there is no data about length of employment in single-person units, it is of interest that Shuter's portrait of 'the "average" OMB' shows someone in post for under three years, while 'the "average" dissatisfied OMB' has been in post a little longer![5]

9.3 Career options for solo information workers

The solo information worker has several options:

- Stay put – enjoy your role and foster your personal development
- Expand the service – *if* there is potential to improve the service by expansion. Assume responsibility for managing new staff, wave farewell to the solo role and make sure you get a promotion
- Use your skills to gain promotion by moving into new areas of practice – and gain appropriate skills and qualifications
- Specialize in developing new one-person units – and accept that this career decision is unlikely to enrich your bank balance
- Seek a post in a larger information unit – benefit from the proximity of fellow information workers. Go in at the top – or give up your autonomy gracefully.

There are other possibilities too. If autonomy is crucial to you, and you have an entrepreneurial spirit, consider freelance work. Of course the possibility of redundancy is a fact of life for the solo librarian, who is prey to the fortunes of the employing organization as well as to internal competition for resources. Anyone seeeking 'pastures new' will find a list of recruitment agencies in Appendix 3.

9.4 Career development

Professional development and career development are not synonymous, although the two are often perceived as such. Nevertheless without the former the latter stands little chance.

Reflection is undoubtedly the most important tool for career planning, and commitment to planned professional development one of its most important features. The need to utilize the 'invisible college', maintain motivation, systematically identify and plan personal development, to use whichever means appropriate to pursue goals, and to monitor progress, has already been explored.

Further reflection may usefully be guided and supplemented by careers publications and short courses. Admittedly there are few books on career development for library and information workers; Trask and Wood's contribution from the Australian context remains a seminal work.[6] However, the wealth of general literature on self-management and career development is relevant, and readers may select from the different approaches used. The Select bibliography gives examples of both specific and general texts, while Appendix 5 illustrates one approach to the process of career development.

9.4.1 — *Personal consistency*

On a cautionary note it is important to be aware of what your career is doing to you, as well as for you. Any run of autobiographies bears testimony to the fact that career development is not entirely rational.

The solo librarian who yearns to be a soloist needs to review life very carefully before making a commitment to long-term goals in information work (see section 6.4.6 on personal SWOT analysis). Former librarians are currently employed in motorsport, as astrologers, trainers, and even 'soft-porn' writers! Sellen's book on *What else you can do with a library degree* may give you other ideas.[7]

9.4.2 — *Formulating alternative strategies*

The most successful career strategy is to take advantage of opportunities by exploiting personal strengths. A different approach is needed when the environment is hostile. Threatened by the advance of computerized circulation systems, the expert in photo-charging was doubtless obliged to overcome weaknesses and remedy gaps in skills in order to find a new role.

9.4.3 — *Reviewing the situation*

The wise manager of a one-person or one-professional unit monitors new developments within their sector of employment, as well as following employment trends within library and information work, using literature and interpersonal networks to keep informed.

Leary and Leary argue that 'We constantly outlive and outgrow aspects of our career;' and that a 'career evolves in cycles'.[8] So it is necessary to keep personal development under review. New aptitudes and interests may emerge and should be integrated into the professional development plan.

9.5 — Preparing for the future

Some people reject the concept of career planning as futile in the face of changing circumstances. Others shy away from it, in the belief that commitment to one goal involves a decisive rejection of another, fearing that planning somehow limits the potential for opportunism. However 'keeping your options open' is at the heart of career planning. As Burrington found, it is 'general planning', focused on the progressive attainment of a series of minor goals, which 'allows people to recognize and take opportunities'.[9]

Preparing for the future by means of planned development opens the door to opportunities, both personal and professional, and strengthens the ability to take advantage of whatever the future holds.

References

1   Brown, R., *A framework for continuing professional development for library and information services staff*, British Library, 1992. British Library R&D Report 6070.
2   Willis, L. and Daisley, J., *Springboard: women's development workbook*, Hawthorn Press, 1990.
3   St Clair, G. and Williamson, J., *Managing the new one-person library*, 2nd edn, Bowker-Saur, 1992.
4   Ritchie, S., *Training and management development in librarianship*, British

Library, 1988. Library and Information Research Report 34.

5   Shuter, J., 'The isolated professional', *Information & library manager*, **3** (4), 1984, 106–13.

6   Trask, M. and Wood, J., *Career planning and assessment for librarians*, Kuring-gai College of Advanced Education, Lindfield, New South Wales, 1984.

7   Sellen, B-C. (ed.), *What else you can do with a library degree*, Gaylord Professional Publications, Syracuse, New York, 1980.

8   Leary, J. and Leary, M., 'Transforming your career', in Pedler, M., Burgoyne, J. and Boydell, T. (eds.), *Applying self-development in organizations*, Prentice Hall, 1988.

9   Burrington, G., *Equally good: women in British librarianship*, AAL Publishing, 1993.

Select bibliography

This selective bibliography offers a 'starting point' for further reading on key areas for professional development for solo librarians and information workers. A look at the range of recent publications from both Aslib and The Library Association is also recommended.

BLISS produces a number of literature guides and will conduct specific searches on request. Further information may be obtained from the British Library Information Sciences Service, 7 Ridgmount Street, London WC1E 7AE. Tel. 0171-323 7688.

Assertiveness

Back, K. and Back, K. with Bates, T., *Assertiveness at work: a practical guide to handling awkward situations*, 2nd edn, McGraw-Hill, 1991.
Caputo, J. S., *The assertive librarian*, Oryx Press, 1984.
Gillen, T., *Assertiveness for managers*, Gower, 1992.
Jones, N. and Jordan, P., *Case studies in library management*, Clive Bingley, 1988, Ch. 11.
Rees, S. and Graham, R., *Assertion training: how to be who you really are*, Routledge, 1991.
Townend, A., *Developing assertiveness*, Routledge, 1991.

Career development

General texts
This list gives examples from the field. Material varies in quality and taste.

Bolles, R. N., *What color is your parachute?: a practical manual for job-hunters and career changers*, Ten Speed Press, Annual.
Francis, D., *Managing your own career*, Harper Collins, 1994.
Kemp, D. and Kemp, F., *The mid career action guide: a practical guide to mid-career change*, Kogan Page, 1991.
Pedler, M., Burgoyne, J. and Boydell, T. (eds.), *Applying self-development in organizations*, Prentice Hall, 1988. Part 3 is concerned with career development and self-development.

Career planning for librarians
Sellen, B-C. (ed.), *What else you can do with a library degree*, Gaylord Professional Publications, 1980.
Slater, M., *Careers guidance and library/information work*, British Library, 1986. Library and Information Research Report 48.
Spivack, J. F. (ed.), *Careers in information*, Knowledge Industry Publications Inc., 1982.
Trask, M. and Wood, J., *Career planning and assessment for librarians*, Kuring-gai College of Advanced Education, Lindfield, New South Wales, 1984.

Evaluation of small libraries

Abbott, C., *Performance measurement in library and information services*, Aslib, 1994.

Cronin, B., 'Performance measurement and information management', *Aslib proceeedings*, **34** (5), May 1982, 227–36.

Jones, N. and Jordan, P., *Case studies in library management*, Clive Bingley, 1988, Ch. 16.

Lancaster, F. W., *If you want to evaluate your library . . .*, 2nd edn, Library Association Publishing, 1993.

McElroy, A. R., 'Library-information service evaluation: a case-history from pharmaceutical R and D', *Aslib proceedings*, May 1982, 249–65.

South West Thames Regional Library Service, *A quality library service: management manual for healthcare libraries*, SWTRLS, 1993. Includes sample tools for monitoring interlibrary loans, reference enquiries and so on.

Strife, M. L., 'Special libraries assessment or marketing the special library', *The reference librarian*, Haworth Press, **17** (38), 1992, 53–6.

Walsh, A., 'All the world is data and we are but ciphers in it . . . William Shakespere 1992', *The reference librarian*, Haworth Press, **17** (38), 1992, 21–30.

Financial management

Northern Training Group/Scottish Council for Educational Technology, *Financial management for librarians: open learning for library staff*, NTG/SCET, 1993.

Information technology

Bawden, D. and Blakeman, K., *Going automated: implementing and using information technology in special libraries and information units*, Aslib, 1990.

Lemaire, K., 'Choosing a school library management system', *SLG news*, **30**, Winter 1993, 3–7.

NB In a field characterized by continual change it is important to consult material which is recent and readable. Both Aslib and The Library Association regularly publish in this field and the School Library Association will gladly recommend appropriate titles (see Appendix 3). In addition the *Library Information Technology Centre* has an extensive publishing programme, for example:

Guide to choosing an automated system, LITC Report no. 2.
Library systems for schools: introductory pack, rev. 1994.

Further details may be obtained from LITC, South Bank Technopark, 90 London Road, London SE1 6LN. Tel. 0171-815 7872.

Learning

Kolb, D. A. and Fry, R., 'Towards an applied theory of experiential learning', in Cooper, C. L. (ed.), *Theories of group processes*, Wiley, 1975.

Mumford, A., 'Enhancing your learning skills – a note of guidance for managers', in Wood, S. (ed.), *Continuous development: the path to improved performance*, Institute of Personnel Management, 1988.

Mumford, A., 'Learning to learn and management of self-development', in Pedler, M., Burgoyne, J. and Boydell, T. (eds.), *Applying self-development in organizations*, Prentice-Hall, 1988.

Orr, F., *How to succeed at part-time study*, Unwin, 1988.

Pont, A. M., *Developing effective training skills*, 1991. See Ch. 4: 'Learning theory'.

Marketing

Cronin, B., *Marketing of library and information services 2*, Aslib, 1992.

Dean, S., *Winning marketing techniques: an introduction to marketing for information professionals*, Special Libraries Association, 1990.

Duncan, M., 'Black and white: the press release as a marketing tool', *Aslib information*, **21** (9), Sept. 1993, 341–3.

Farber Sirkin, A. F., 'Marketing planning for maximum effectiveness', *Special libraries*, **82** (1), Winter 1991, 1–6.

Prytherch, R. (ed.), *Handbook of library training practice*, Vol.2, Gower, 1990. Ch. 3.

Smith, A., 'Marketing – what is it all about?', *Aslib information*, **21** (9), Sept. 1993, 334.

St Clair, G., 'Marketing and promotion in today's special library', *Aslib proceedings*, **42** (7/8), July/Aug. 1990, 213–17.

Planning

Webb, S. P., 'Planning for success: an outline', in Foreman, L., *Change in libraries and information services*, Circle of State Librarians, HMSO, 1993.

Professional development

General texts

Everard, K. B. (ed.), *Development training – progress and prospects: the development of personal, group and community effectiveness*, Development Training Advisory Group, 1987.

Institute of Personnel and Development, *CPD policy: a vehicle for learning*, IPD, 1995.

Todd, F. (ed.), *Planning continuing professional development*, Croom Helm, 1987.

Wood, S. (ed.), *Continuous development: the path to improved performance*, Institute of Personnel Management, 1988.

Librarianship and information work

Brown, R., *A framework for continuing professional development for library and information services staff*, British Library Research & Development Department, 1992. British Library R&D Report 6070.

Layzell Ward, P. (ed.), *The professional development of the librarian and information worker*, Aslib, 1980.

McElroy, R., 'The unwritten contract: personal professional development', *SLA news*, No. 177, Sept.–Oct. 1983, 27–33.

Roberts, N. and Konn, T., *Librarians and professional status: continuing professional development and academic libraries*, Library Association Publishing, 1991.

Webb, S. P., *Personal development in information work*, 2nd edn, Aslib, 1991.

Weingand, D., 'Continuing education', *Journal of education for librarianship*, **24** (4), 1984, 278–82.

Woolley, M., 'The one-person library: professional development and professional management', *Library management*, **9** (1), 1988.

The professional portfolio

Institute of Personnel and Development, *Personal action plan and CPD record*, IPD, 1995. This is one alternative means of recording achievement to Stage 6 (A) of The Library Association's *Your personal profile*.

The Library Association, *The framework for continuing professional development: your personal profile*, The Library Association, 1992.

Redman, W., *Portfolios for development: a guide for trainers and managers*, Kogan Page, 1994.

Setting up a one-person library and information service

Jones, N. and Jordan, P., *Case studies in library management*, Clive Bingley, 1988, Ch. 16.

St Clair, G. and Williamson, J., *Managing the new one-person library*, 2nd edn, Bowker-Saur, 1992. This book includes chapters on financial management, information technology and marketing.

Webb, S. P., *Creating an information service*, 2nd edn, Aslib, 1988.

Statistics

Simpson, I. S., *How to interpret statistical data: a guide for librarians and information scientists*, The Library Association, 1990.

Time management

Berner, A., *Time management in the small library: a self-study program*, Special Libraries Association, 1988.

Burgin, R. and Hansel, P., 'Library management: a dialogue. Time on our side', *Wilson library bulletin*, Sept. 1990, 63–5.

Lankford, M. D., 'The race against time: winning strategies for librarians', *School library journal*, **39** (8), Aug. 1993, 28–32.

Moon, P., *The time-management workbook: an opportunity to review your working practices and make better use of time*, Headway Training and Development, 1990.

Whitehall, T., 'Time to think – use of the systems approach to the problems of the "one-man" information unit', *Aslib proceedings*, **19** (12), Dec. 1967, 406–15.

Appendix 1
An information network: health education

Academic institutions
e.g. college library
    university library

National bodies
e.g. College of Health
    King's Fund

Professional bodies
e.g. Association of Public Health
    Health Visitors Association
    Institute of Health Education
    Royal College of Nursing
    Society of Health Education
    and Health Promotion
    Specialists

HEALTH EDUCATOR
e.g. care worker, environmental health officer,
health promotion officer, health visitor,
parent, teacher, youth worker

Local authority
e.g. council – voluntary service
    environmental health dept.
    multicultural centre
    public libraries
    social services
    teachers' centre
    youth service

National Health Service
Nationally
e.g. dept. of health
    health education authority

Locally
e.g. community health council
    district health authority
    drug information pharmacist
    health promotion unit
    medical library – postgraduate
        centre
    nursing library
    regional healthline

Advisory agencies
e.g. Citizens Advice Bureau
    Community Relations Council

Voluntary sector
e.g. Age Concern, MIND, SANDS,
    TACADE

For further information see Lacey Bryant, S., 'Exploiting the information
network in support of health education', *Journal of the Institute of Health
Education*, **25** (4), 1987, 132–9.

Appendix 2
Croydon Health Information Providers (CHIPs): Sources of Health Information in Croydon

THE DISTRICT LIBRARY SERVICE

Health Promotion Library

WHO CAN USE OUR SERVICE?

Professionals and students in Croydon working in health promotion and health related fields, and, for reference, to members of the public.

WHERE WE ARE?

Croydon Health Promotion Library
Carshalton and Croydon College of Nursing and Midwifery Library
100 London Road
Croydon   CR9 2 RH
Telephone Number   081-684-6999

Open: 9.00-5.00 Monday, Tuesday, Wednesday & Friday
       9.00-5.00 Alternate Thursdays
Staff: Health Promotion Librarian (part-time)
        Assistant Librarian (part-time)

SOME TYPICAL ENQUIRIES:

1. Information on Health Promotion theory and practice.
2. Specific queries on Health Promotion issues.
3. Information on a disease, drug or syndrome.
4. Queries on general health and social issues.
5. Information on local and national support and self-help groups.

RESOURCES AVAILABLE

We have a variety of resources for different needs:

1. Book Stock
   - Specialist and popular texts
   - Small reference collection
   - Teaching packs

2. Information Files
   - Topic files
   - Local information files

3. Journals
   - Health promotion
   - Public health
   - General health & social issues

4. Inter Library Loans
   - photocopies
   - loans

5. Catalogues
   - All books held in South West Thames Regional Libraries, on microfiche, by author, title and subject.

Croydon Health Information Providers, *Sources of health information in Croydon*, CHIPs, nd. Reproduced with permission

Appendix 3
Organizations

Professional associations

International
See Riss Fang, A. and Songe, A. with Herz, A., *World guide to library, archives and information science associations*, Saur, 1990. IFLA publication 52/53.

United Kingdom
Aslib
The Association for Information
  Management
20–24 Old Street
London EC1V 9AP
Tel: 0171-253 4488

Institute of Information Scientists
44–45 Museum Street
London WC1A 1LY
Tel: 0171-831 8003/8633

The Library Association
7 Ridgmount Street
London WC1E 7AE
Tel: 0171-636 7543

The School Library Association
Liden Library
Barrington Close
Liden
Swindon SN3 6HF
Tel: 01793 617838

United States of America
American Library Association
50 East Huron Street
Chicago
Illinois 60611
USA

Special Libraries Association
1700 18th Street
NW Washington
DC 20009
USA

Qualifications: sources of further information

Distance learning
Information North
Bolbec Hall
Westgate Road
Newcastle upon Tyne NE1 1SE
Tel: 0191-232 0877

The Open University
Walton Hall
Milton Keynes
Bucks MK7 6AA

Society of Indexers
38 Rochester Road
London NW1 9JJ
Tel: 0171-916 7809

Department of Information and
  Library Studies
University of Wales
Llanbadarn Fawr
Aberystwyth
Dyfed SY23 3AS
Tel: 01970 622188/623111

Paraprofessional qualifications

Details of qualifications for library and information assistants (such as those awarded by City and Guilds, BTEC and SCOTVEC) may be obtained from:

The Library Association
7 Ridgmount Street
London WC1E 7AE
Tel: 0171-636 7543

Professional qualifications
The Library Association (see above) and the Institute of Information Scientists provide information regarding those courses which are recognized for the attainment of their professional qualifications:

Institute of Information Scientists
44–45 Museum Street
London WC1A 1LY
Tel: 0171-831 8003/8633

Recruitment agencies

Aardvark Information and Library
Personnel
1 Railway Approach
London Bridge
London SE1 9SL
Tel: 0171-357 0666

Bellwater Ltd
Rivington House
82 Great Eastern Street
London EC2A 3JL
Tel: 0171-729 1566

Informed Recruitment Services
25 Old Street
London EC1V 9HL
Tel: 0171-490 2811

TFPL Recruitment
17–18 Britton Street
London EC1M 5NQ
Tel: 0171-251 5522

Aslib Professional Recruitment
Limited
Information House
20–24 Old Street
London EC1V 9AP
Tel: 0171-253 4488

INFOmatch
The Library Association
7 Ridgmount Street
London WC1E 7AE
Tel: 0171-636 7543

Instant Library Recruitment
1 Rectory Place
Loughborough LE11 1UW
Tel: 01509 268292

Unique Recruitment Services Ltd
61 Cheapside
London EC2V 6AX
Tel: 0171-489 9639

Training providers

Training agencies
These agencies are among those which offer training tailored to meet the needs of library and information workers.

Burrington Partnership
33 Green Courts
Bowdon
Altrincham
Cheshire WA14 2SR
Tel: 0161-928 6240

Information Unlimited
Clifton House
31 Solihull Road
Shirley
Solihull
West Midlands B90 3HB
Tel: 0121-744 4318

Capital Planning Information Ltd
52 High Street
St Martin's
Stamford
Lincs PE9 2LG
Tel: 01780 57300

TFPL Ltd
17–18 Britton Street
London EC1M 5NQ
Tel: 0171-251 5522

Other training organizations: examples

Institute of Personnel and
  Development
IPD House
Camp Road
London SW19 4UX
Tel: 0181-946 9100

The Tavistock Institute
30 Tabernacle Street
London EC2A 4DE
Tel: 0171-417 8310

Many organizations outside the information sector offer excellent, relevant training. Regrettably the fees charged by the better known organizations (especially those offering management training) are generally beyond the resources which most solo information workers can command.

Local training bodies: examples

Courses organized at a local level tend to be relatively inexpensive. While these specific examples are named in the text (see section 7.7.3), their equivalent will be found in most localities, along with a range of other training providers.

Adult Continuing Education
Area Office
Quarrendon Centre
Holman Street
Aylesbury
Bucks HP19 3LJ

Beds & Bucks Information
Building 33
Cranfield Institute of Technology
Cranfield
Beds MK43 0AL

Aylesbury College
Oxford Road
Aylesbury
Bucks HP21 8PD

Chiltern Christian Training
  Programme
Chinnor Road
Bledlow Ridge
High Wycombe
Bucks HP14 4AJ

Thames Valley CCi Training Ltd
Tooks Court
Lincolns Inn
Lincoln Road
High Wycombe
Bucks HP12 3RE

Appendix 4
Core skills for library and information work

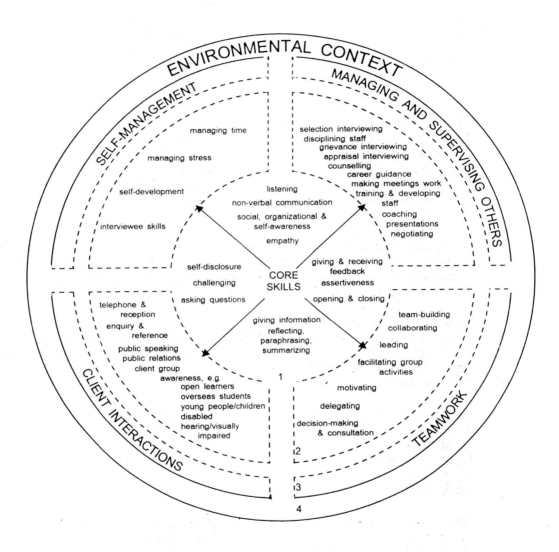

Zone 1   Core skills
Zone 2   Applications
Zone 3   Skills in library and information context
Zone 4   Environmental context

Levy, P., *Interpersonal skills*, Library Association Publishing, 1993.
Reproduced with permission

Appendix 5
Formulation of career strategy

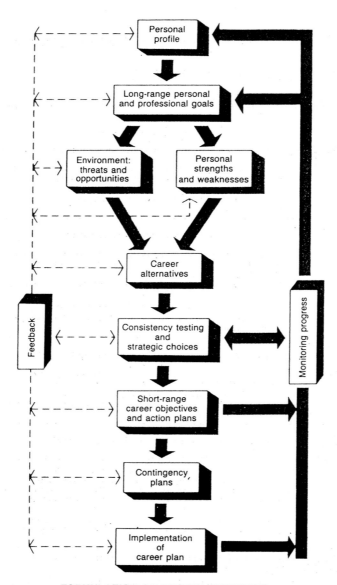

FORMULATION OF CAREER STRATEGY.

Reproduced with permission from McGraw-Hill, Inc. from Weihrich, H. and Koontz, H., *Management: a global perspective*, 10th edn, International edition, McGraw-Hill, Inc., Copyright 1993.

Appendix 6
The Library Association *Framework for continuing professional development:* Guidelines for individuals

1. GUIDELINES FOR INDIVIDUALS

The purpose of this guideline is to enable individuals to exercise personal responsibility for taking appropriate action to establish and maintain intellectual and personal development relevant to current employment and anticipated future work.

ACTION   Show commitment to continuing professional development (CPD).

Good Practice
- Consult *LA Code of Professional Conduct*. Register with appropriate professional bodies. Participate in CPD activities organised by employer, academic institutions or professional bodies.
- Attend professional meetings. Seek involvement in Library Association local branch or special interest group activities.

ACTION   Identify personal needs for continuing professional development.

Good Practice
- Use an approved document (see personal profile) to assist in planning to meet the needs of the individual's job and career and to contribute to the employing organisation's performance.
- Take account of relevant needs and opportunities in the employing organisation together with personal interests and aspirations.
- Take account of any recommendations from relevant professional bodies.
- If currently unemployed use the ideas in the approved document to help in planning a systematic approach to CPD.

ACTION   Develop a personal continuing professional development plan.

Good Practice
- Discuss CPD proposals with the employer, where appropriate using any existing performance appraisal/career development system.
- Obtain information/advice from the employer/ colleague or professional body. Agree the personal CPD plan with the employer, together with their role and support in carrying out the planned actions.

ACTION   Implement the continuing professional development plan.

Good Practice
- Wherever possible ensure that CPD contributes to job performance within 12 months.
- Determine in conjunction with the employer the appropriate amount of CPD to be carried out. As a guide (based on existing good practice) in each year, a range between 28-42 hours, (the equivalent of 4-6 average working days) of CPD activities is recommended. It should be noted that best practice already exceeds this figure. A proportion of this time will always be own-time learning.
- A variety of learning methods should be used depending on the particular learning objectives; the cost-effectiveness of different activities; the preferred learning style of the individual.

ACTION   Record continuing professional development activities, review position and assess benefits.

Good Practice
- Jointly examine with the employer the effectiveness and value of CPD to the individual and the employer. Agree further action.

27

The Library Association, *The framework for continuing professional development: your personal profile*, The Library Association, 1992. Reproduced with permission.

Appendix 7
The Library Association *Framework for continuing professional development*: Stage 1. Element A

STAGE 1. Element A

PRESENT JOB

The aim of this part is to identify where action is needed to contribute to maintaining and improving present job performance.

On the form opposite you should analyse your job taking into account the following questions:

- **What are the key areas which you need in your present job?**

- **For each area, what are the needs for improvements to ensure you carry out your present job effectively?**

- **What improvements are necessary to fill the gaps (in terms of additional knowledge and skills needed)?**

- **How will new technology and other changes affect your job?**

KEY AREAS OF WORK:

This is what you aim to achieve at work: it is why your job exists and what your employer thinks important. Refer to the job description if applicable.

You may find it helpful to break down your job into four areas:

- (a) Library and information skills
- (b) Personal effectiveness/communications
- (c) Management skills
- (d) Corporate skills

KNOWLEDGE AND SKILLS NEEDED

These arise out of your work areas. Take into account:

- The objectives of your job as well as what you actually do.
- Your strengths and abilities which could be built on and developed.
- Areas where help is needed to increase effectiveness.

Try to be as specific as you can in terms of the knowledge and skills needed. You may find it helpful to consider the following lists with reference to the areas above; add to them or amend as necessary.

Library and information skills

- Identify needs of those to be served
- Meeting user needs and demands
- Customer care
- Organising knowledge and information
- Retrieving knowledge and information
- Sources of information
- New developments in products, processes and services

Personal effectiveness

- Problem solving
- Verbal communications
- Written communications
- Coaching
- Teamwork

Management skills

- Planning
- Finance/budgeting
- Personnel/staff management
- Leadership
- Marketing
- Performance review

Corporate skills

- Achieving goals and objectives of parent organisation through library and information services
- Using the organisational context
- Awareness of national and local policies
- Political know-how

6

TRAINING FRAMEWORK CAREER EDUCATION THE LIBRARY ASSOCIATION

STAGE 1.

ELEMENT A	PRESENT JOB
Main work areas	Additional knowledge and skills needed

7

The Library Association, *The framework for continuing professional development: your personal profile*, The Library Association, 1992. Reproduced with permission.

Appendix 8
The Library Association *Framework for continuing professional development*: Stage 1. Element B

STAGE 1. Element B

FUTURE ROLES

The aim of this part is to anticipate changes in your future role(s) at work and to identify areas where action is needed to meet these changes.

On the form opposite analyse your job over the foreseeable future, say up to three years ahead.

- **What areas of your work are likely to change?**

- **What additional knowledge and skills would you have to acquire in order to meet those needs?**

- **Are any job moves possible to make better use of your abilities?**

CHANGING AREAS OF WORK

Refer to the notes in Element A. It would be useful to consider likely changes in both your current job and additional roles you foresee for yourself. The focus should be on those areas of work in which you anticipate changes arising from technology, systems, work patterns, client needs and other factors.

ADDITIONAL KNOWLEDGE AND SKILLS

Refer to the notes in Element A.

8

TRAINING FRAMEWORK CAREER EDUCATION THE LIBRARY ASSOCIATION

STAGE 1.

ELEMENT B	FUTURE ROLES
Changing areas of work	Additional knowledge and skills

9

The Library Association, *The framework for continuing professional development: your personal profile*, The Library Association, 1992. Reproduced with permission.

Appendix 9
American Library Association, SCOLE
Guidelines for quality in continuing education

1.2 Individualized Programs and Activities

The Criteria for Group Programs and Activities (p. 4) and Instructional Materials (p. 9) are applicable to individualized continuing education learning activities. In applying the Criteria to the design and accomplishment of an individualized continuing education activity, special attention must be given to the following additional points:

1.2.1 Needs Assessment

Criterion: **The individual's specific learning needs or interests have been identified and assessed.**

Assessment Factors:

(1) Has an appropriate needs assessment process been followed?
(2) What are needs or interests based upon, e.g. job, career growth, personal interest, etc.?
(3) Are colleagues consulted or outside resources utilized in determining needs?

1.2.2 Objectives

Criterion: **Based on the needs assessment, a set of clear, measurable, and/or observable learning objectives have been stated in one or more of the following areas: changes in attitudes; updating of outdated knowledge and/or attainment of new knowledge; and awareness or mastery of specific skills and techniques.**

Assessment Factors:

(1) Are the objectives clearly stated?
(2) Are the objectives appropriate in meeting the assessed needs?
(3) Will the objectives contribute to the competence of the individual?
(4) Are the objectives reasonable and attainable given the individual's current expertise and the available resources and time?
(5) Do the objectives specify the expected outcome for the individual in terms of the level of knowledge or performance that is expected to be attained?
(6) Are the objectives stated in measurable terms so that they can be evaluated? How will the individual know or be able to demonstrate achievement of each objective?
(7) Do the objectives address changes in future role performance of the individual as a basis for evaluating impact?

1.2.3 Learning Plan

Criterion: **An organized and coherent series of learning activities is systematically planned to achieve the individual's stated objectives.**

Assessment Factors:

(1) Are learning activities appropriate to the objectives?
(2) Do the activities utilize appropriate materials, resources, or persons expert in the content/skill area?
(3) Are learning activities organized, sequenced, and paced so as to be manageable and to build effectively upon each other?
(4) Are appropriate and effective educational strategies/techniques employed that respond to the individual's learning style?
(5) Are the activities at the appropriate level for the individual's level of competence?
(6) Is adequate time allocated to achievement of the objectives of each activity?

1.2.4 Evaluation

Criterion: Evaluation is an on-going and integral part of the individualized continuing education activity.

Assessment Factors:

(1) Is the evaluation based on the stated objectives?
(2) Has the plan of activities been followed?
(3) Does the evaluation cover the starting point, the process, and the outcomes of the learning experience?
(4) Does monitoring provide opportunity for reassessment of objectives and adjustment of the program in light of newly realized needs/interests or unrealistic expectations?
(5) Are resources and experts utilized as planned?
(6) Do the monitoring and evaluation look at appropriateness of the content and resources and the effectiveness of learning strategies?
(7) Do monitoring and evaluation effectively assess the individual's level of achievement of the objectives and provide opportunity for corrective efforts?
(8) Does the evaluation encourage application of learning to the work situation?
(9) Is the monitoring and evaluation process carried out with appropriate review, assessment, or consultation with a qualified, unbiased person?

Continuing Education Subcommittee of the Standing Committee on Library Education (SCOLE), *Guidelines for quality in continuing education for information, library and media personnel*, ALA, 1988. Reproduced with permission.

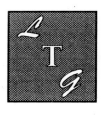

Appendix 10
Examples of training material: assertion and time management

 Assertion

Trainer: Sue Germain

Guidelines on assertive discussion

Do:

- select a mutually convenient time when all participants can give their full attention;
- be clear about what you want to say; have objectives and goals; be confident in your approach;
- know what outcome is acceptable to you, what isn't, and where you can be flexible;
- when putting your case, be sure to say what the positive benefits of what you want are;
- remain calm;
- ignore attempts by others to divert conversation away from the issue;
- commit your thinking to paper if appropriate;
- know relevant facts/rights/subject matter;
- at the close, finish – don't hover.

Don't:

- use threats;
- be diffident;
- apologize unnecessarily;
- divert away from the issue;
- ask permission or see yourself as a victim, e.g. when speaking about a right or an entitlement don't say 'Is it alright if . . . ';
- give the impression the outcome is fine for you when it is not;
- think you have reached the end of the road if you don't succeed in getting what you want. There may well be other avenues and pathways open to you.

Sue Germain, Counsellor and Trainer, may be contacted via: 23 Western Road, Wolverton, Milton Keynes, Bucks MK12 5AY. Tel: 01908 226909.

Time management

Trainer: Joan Williamson

RUNNING A ONE-PERSON LIBRARY EFFECTIVELY

Regardless of how well-qualified and experienced you think you are, you will never run a one-person information unit effectively if you don't take note of the following self-help rules:

Do not waste time complaining about problems

Accept your limitations - no one is perfect

Be friendly to your users

Keep calm and never panic - behaving like a headless chicken is not constructive!

Think about your task more than once if you need to, but only DO it once

View any problems as opportunities and don't just solve them - exploit them as as well

If you have a problem, do something about it NOW - don't procrastinate.

Do not pursue lost causes

Do not make excuses

Don't say you will try to do something on time, just do it!

Do not look for difficulties - they may never come up

Start something new each day

Finish something each day - that way you go home in a positive mood

Keep outside activities out of work

Be on time and keep appointments

Do the hardest jobs earliest in the day when your energy is highest

Use selective delays; stop sometimes and think about the specific job you are doing at the moment.

Do not miss deadlines

Be honest with yourself and others - seek help if you do not know how to do something yourself

Budget well

Be composed

Bring any conflect out into the open

Improve your learning, concentration and reading skills

Recognise stress and learn how to cope with it

Avoid alcohol during the day . Be aware of side effects of any medication which you may be taking.

Stay fit

Develop a confidant or mentor - you need someone to talk to

Don't be lazy

Avoid negative or destructive thinking

MAINTAIN A SENSE OF HUMOUR!!

Recognise that you **CAN** do more than one thing at a time

Ask others how they manage time. Everyone has their own ideas about time management

And most important of all - **NETWORK** with other information experts for all you are worth! A short phone-call to a colleague to pick their brains could save you hours of brainfade and re-invention of the wheel!

REMEMBER the three RRR's and be   **RESOLUTE**
                                                  RESOURCEFUL
                                                  READY   for anything!

Mrs J. B. Williamson may be contacted via:

Clubhouse Librarian
The Royal Automobile Club
89 Pall Mall
London SW1Y 5HS
Tel: 0171-930 2345 (daytime)

37 Brackley Road
Beckenham
Kent BR3 1RB

Tel: 0181-658 1462 (evenings)

Appendix 11
Kolb's experiential learning cycle

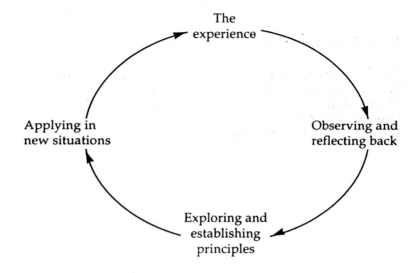

The
experience

Observing and
reflecting back

Exploring and
establishing
principles

Applying in
new situations

Levy, P., *Interpersonal skills*, Library Association Publishing, 1993.
Reproduced with permission.

Index